SPACED OUT

PUNCH
among the Galaxies

Edited by William Hewison

A PUNCH BOOK
Published in association with
GRAFTON BOOKS
A Division of the Collins Publishing Group

LONDON GLASGOW
TORONTO SYDNEY AUCKLAND

Grafton Books
A Division of the Collins Publishing Group
8 Grafton Street, London W1X 3LA

Published by Grafton Books 1987

British Library Cataloguing in Publication Data

Spaced out: Punch among the galaxies
1. Outer space – Caricatures and cartoons
2. English wit and humor, Pictorial
I. Hewison, William – II. Punch
741.5'942 NC1476

ISBN 0-246-13239-6

Printed in Great Britain by
William Collins Sons & Co. Ltd, Glasgow

Introduction

'We can't go on meeting like this'; 'Darling, they're playing our tune'; 'And this is my husband's little den.' Three remarks which don't at first seem to have much in common; yet – at least to those of us who have watched the antics of cartoonists over a decade or two – they fit snugly together into a single, clearly defined compartment. Each of them is a caption cliché. Each of them, by some peculiar accident, is a phrase to which cartoonists have fixed umpteen different scenarios, umpteen variations. The drawing is fresh, the caption remains the same.

A fourth candidate for inclusion in that compartment would certainly be 'Take me to your leader.' That one is perhaps the daddy of them all, a caption which has spawned a multifarious and mind-boggling array of situations, even in the end becoming a free-standing catchphrase in its own right. I suppose initially it harked back to those exploration, adventure stories in the Rider Haggard mould, so it was a certain cartoonist's back-reference to this source that gave the phrase an altogether fresh lease of life when he produced the first Martian/Flying Saucer cartoon. That cartoonist was Alex Graham, and I hope you won't accuse me of cheating when I reveal that Graham's caption was not 'Take me to your leader', but 'Take us to your President.' His drawing in the *New Yorker* showed a flying-saucer in a field and two bug-eyed Martians talking to a horse. Afterwards, jokesmiths everywhere hurried to get in on the act, and *President* gave way to *leader*, perhaps as a way through to a wider audience.

Robot Martians said it to petrol pumps, gnomic Martians said it to Harold Macmillan on a grouse moor (a neat one, that – Macmillan *was* the British leader at the time), and yet another Martian rang the bell at Franz Schubert's door and demanded to be taken to the composer's *lieder.* And no doubt – though I haven't yet come across it – a cartoon exists somewhere which gathers together a pop-eyed Venusian, a smirking swan and a recently ravished Leda. All in all, 'Take me to your leader' has had a pretty good run for its money.

That's not the full story, though – cartoonists, once they have latched on to a productive theme, will shanghai it towards fresh locations and push it into new alignments. The Unidentified Flying Object and its crew of little green men are therefore liable to turn up anywhere and everywhere, and in all kinds of shapes, in order to act out another humorous situation; Noel Ford has a child-Martian playing with little slabs of stone and the result is

Stonehenge; Haldane's Martians are left with five million digital watches on their hands. This is humorous drawing as a form of science fiction, of course, but sci-fi fantasy is not anarchic – it has its own kind of logic, and the best cartoons of the genre are those which stick to the rules.

Mind, this collection is not just UFOs and humanoid Venusians with stalks on their heads. It also takes account of the traffic the other way: the *real* existence of rocketry and space travel; the moon landings; orbiting astronauts and space walks. They're all taken care of in the following pages, proof that *Punch* cartoonists are no sluggards when it comes to sheer inventiveness. They all have Lift-Off, with All Systems, Go.

William Hewison
March 1987

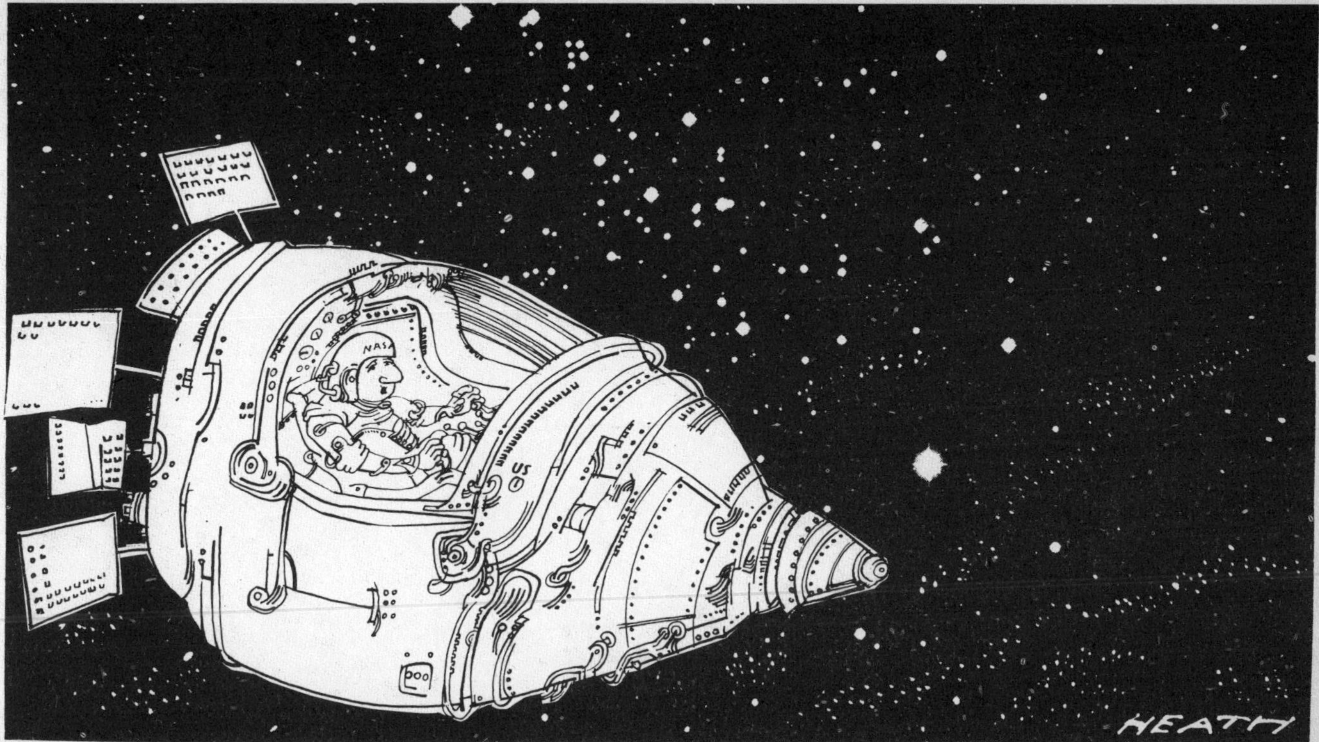

"Sorry, ground control, could you repeat that? I was miles away."

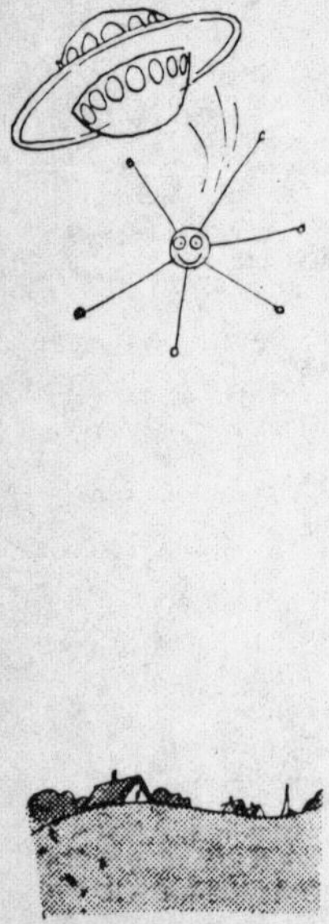

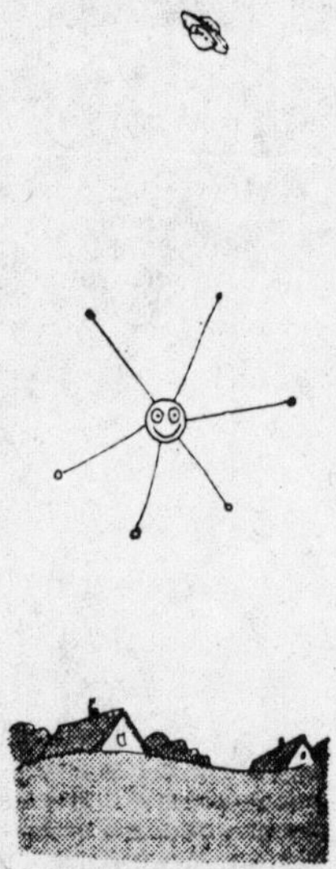

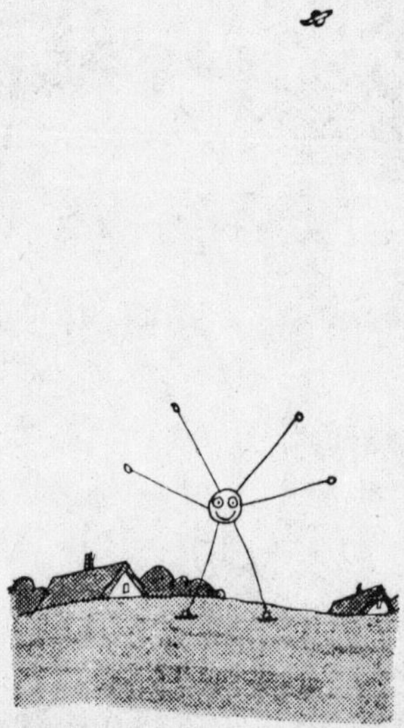

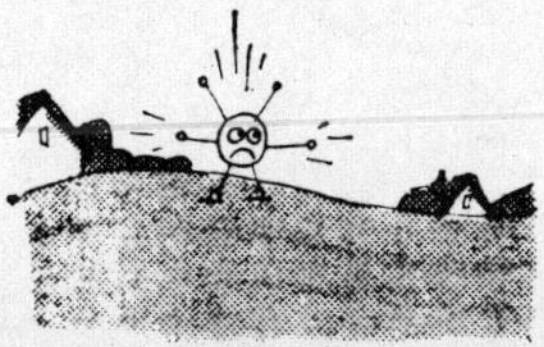

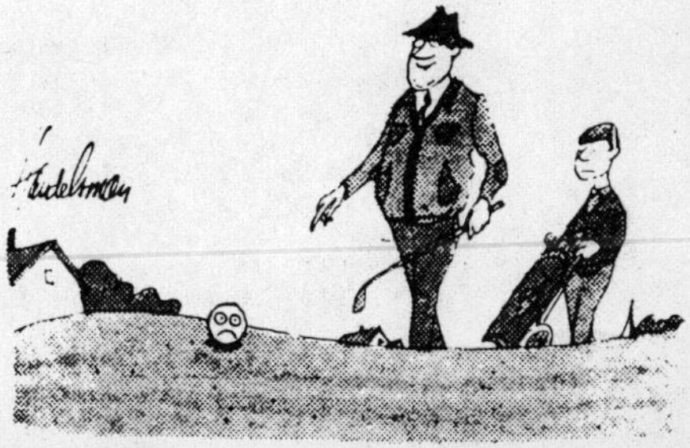

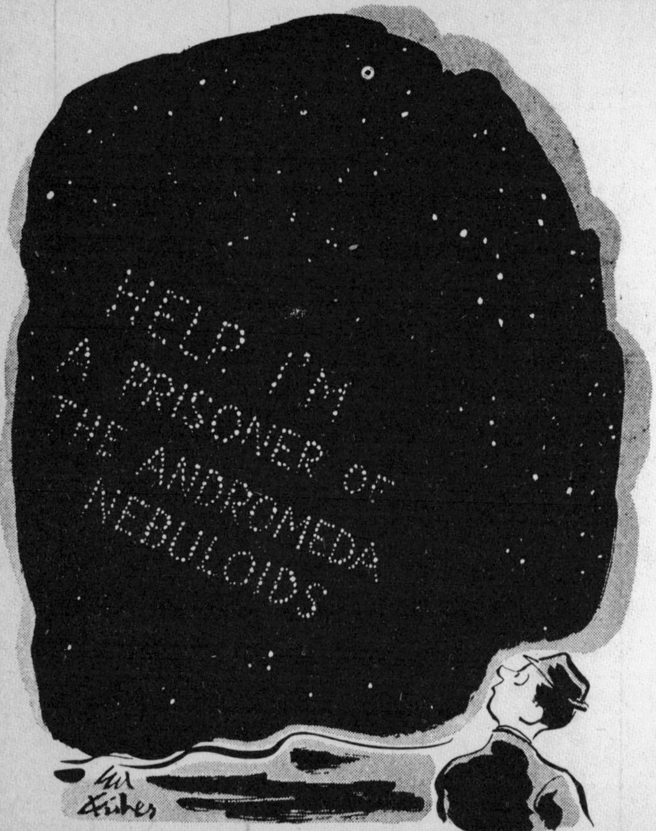

"Hello! The plot thickens!"

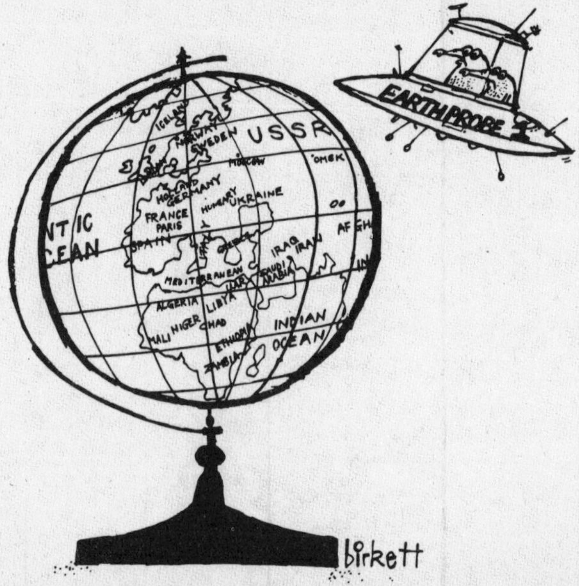

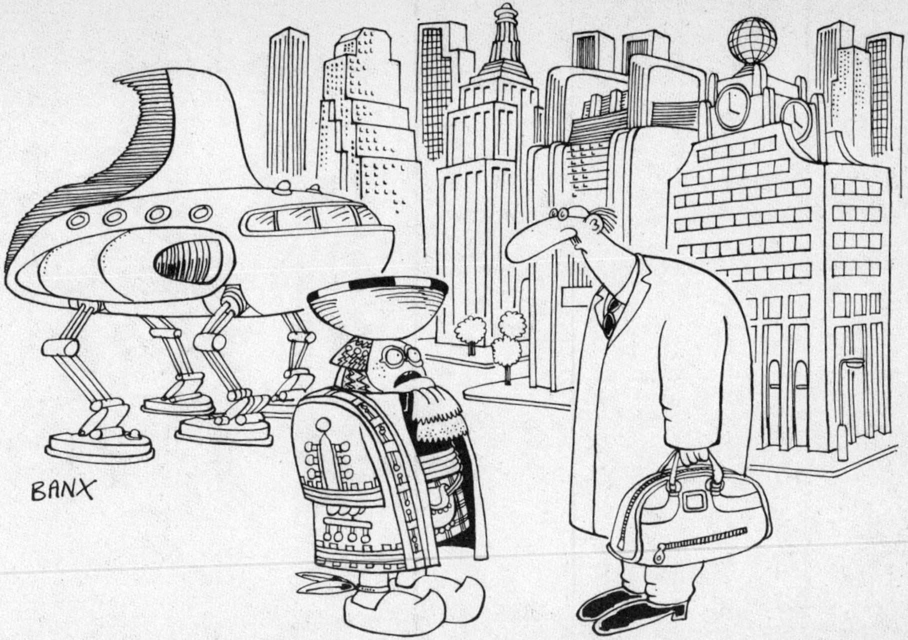

"Well, seeing as you ask, this is the National Costume of Uranus."

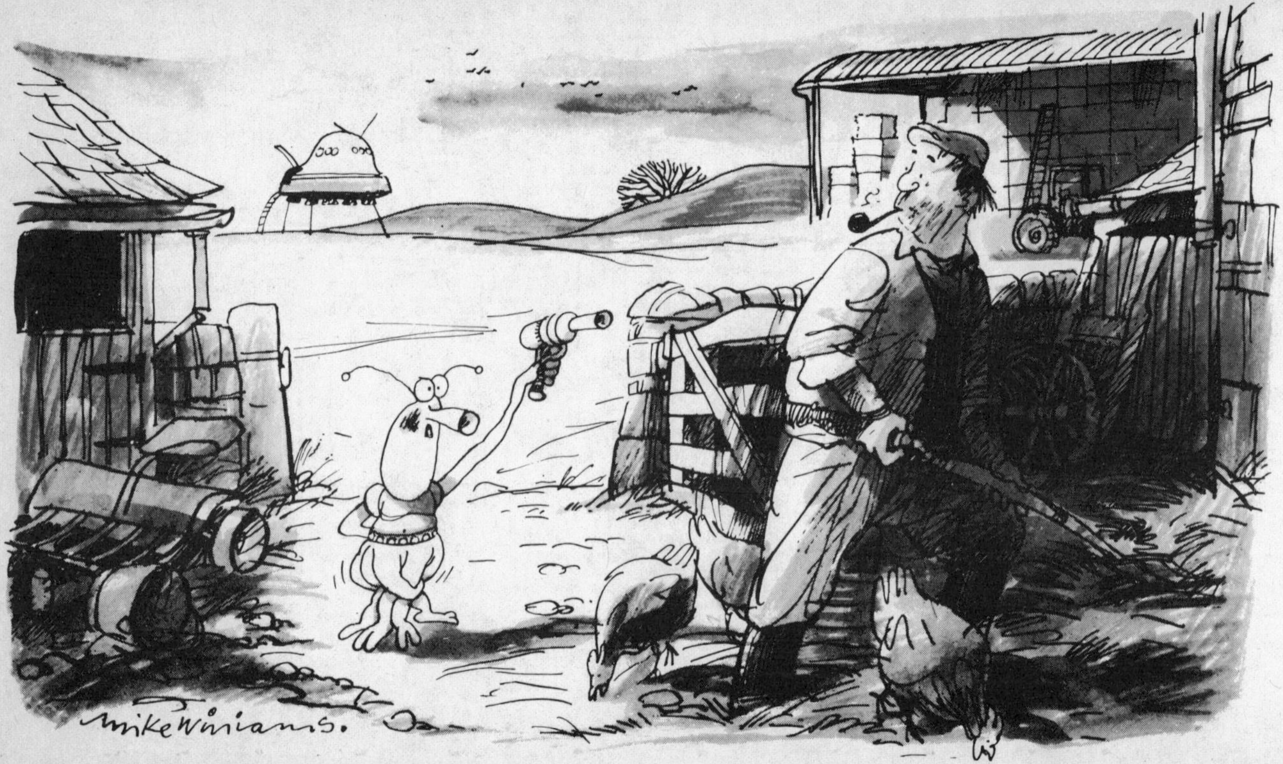

"I am Igsprx from the planet Thynog – take me to your toilet."

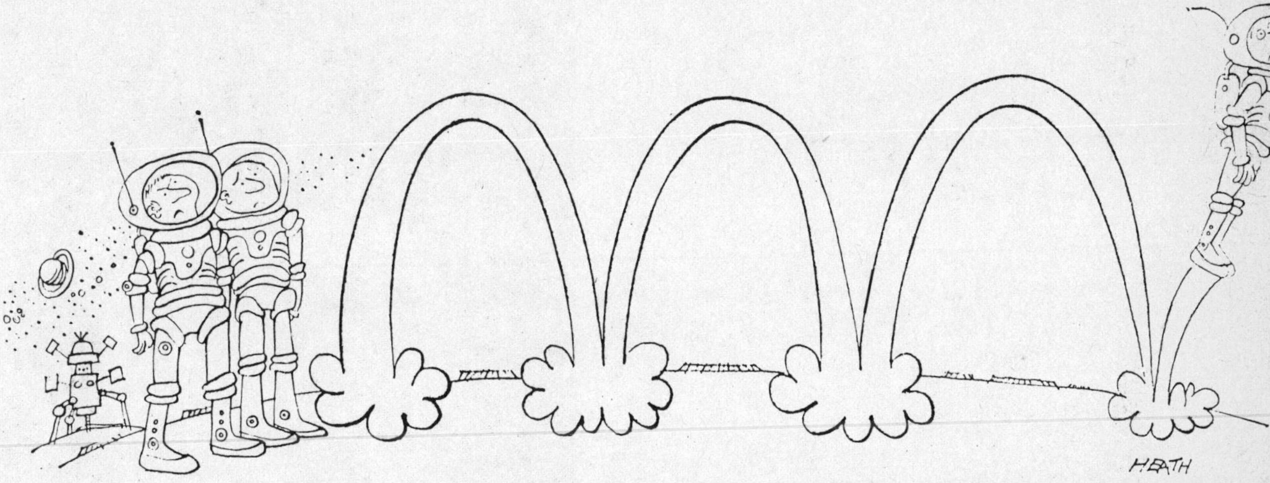

"Hiccups can be a horrible thing up here, Carter!"

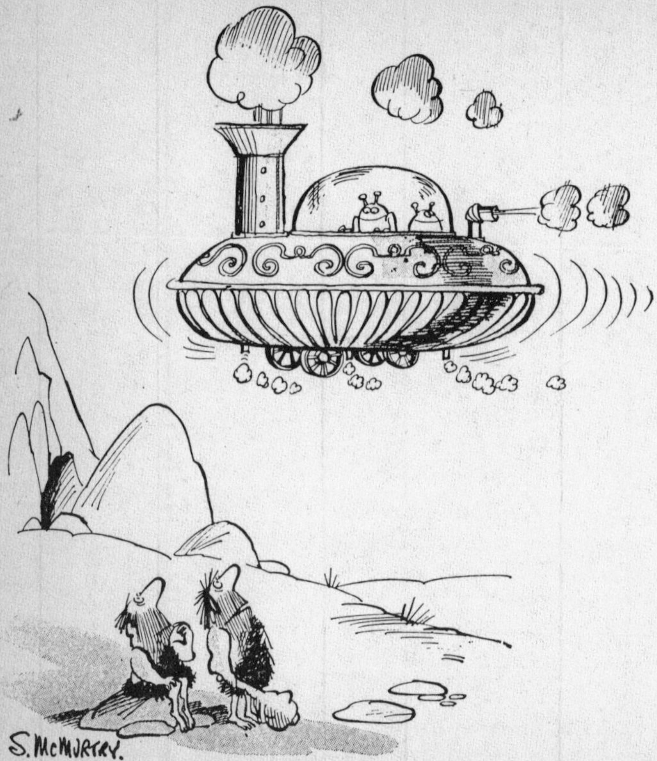

"It's another of those flying saucer things."

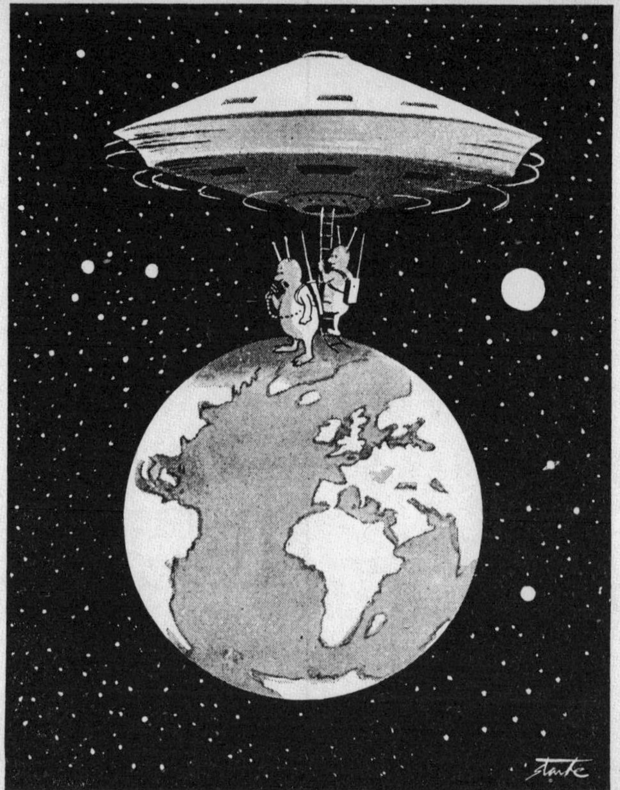
"Calling Jupiter. Calling Jupiter... Reporting from lifeless asteroid. Over to you – over."

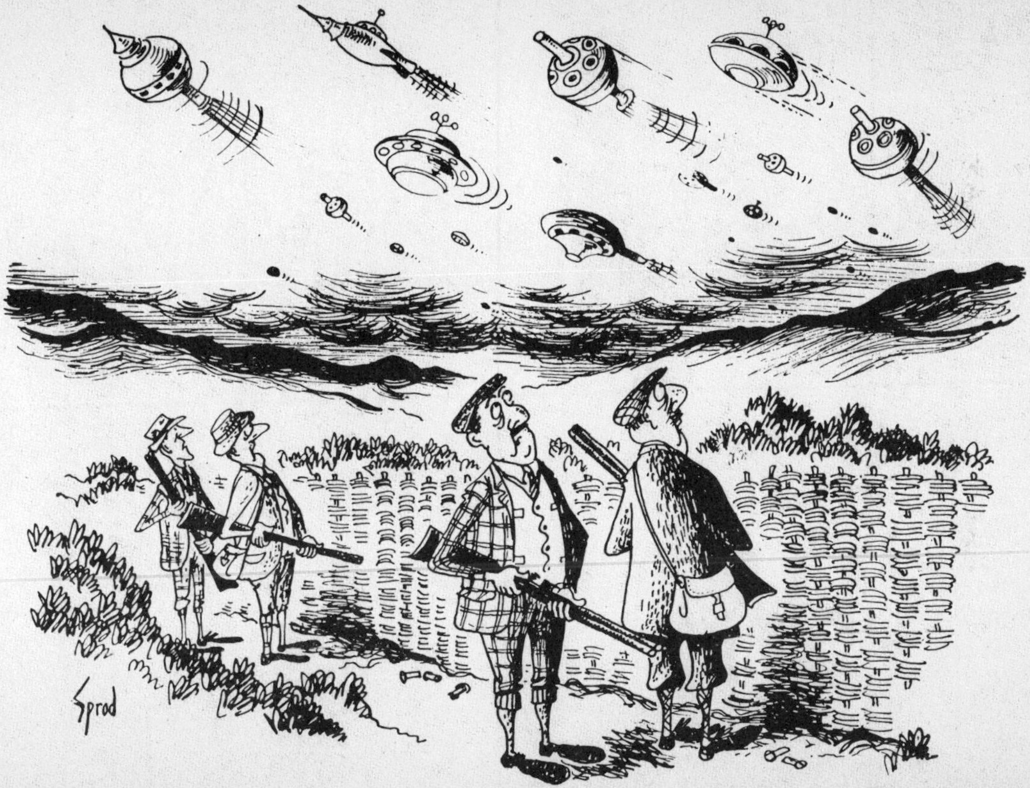

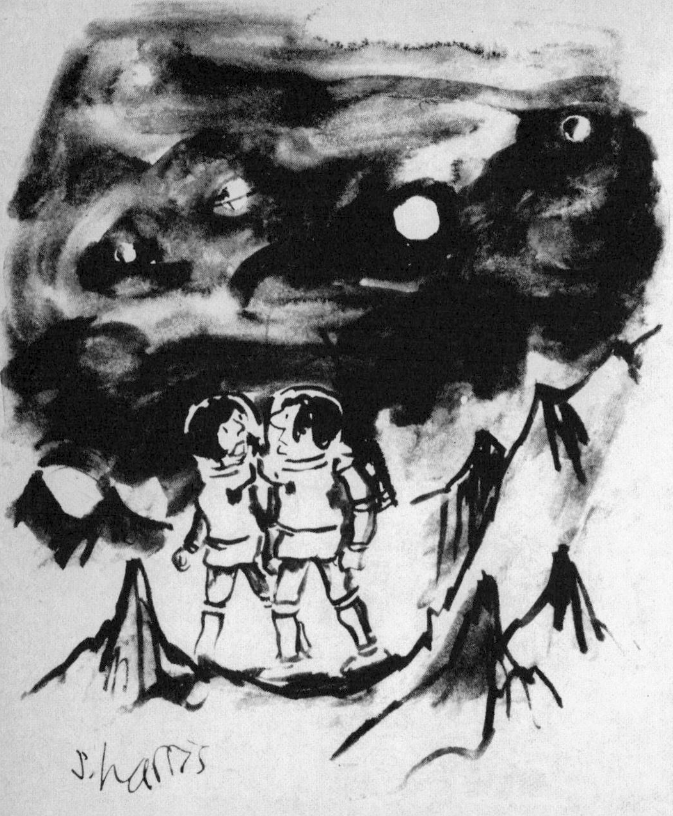

"Sure, I love you, but what kind of neighbourhood is this to bring up kids?"

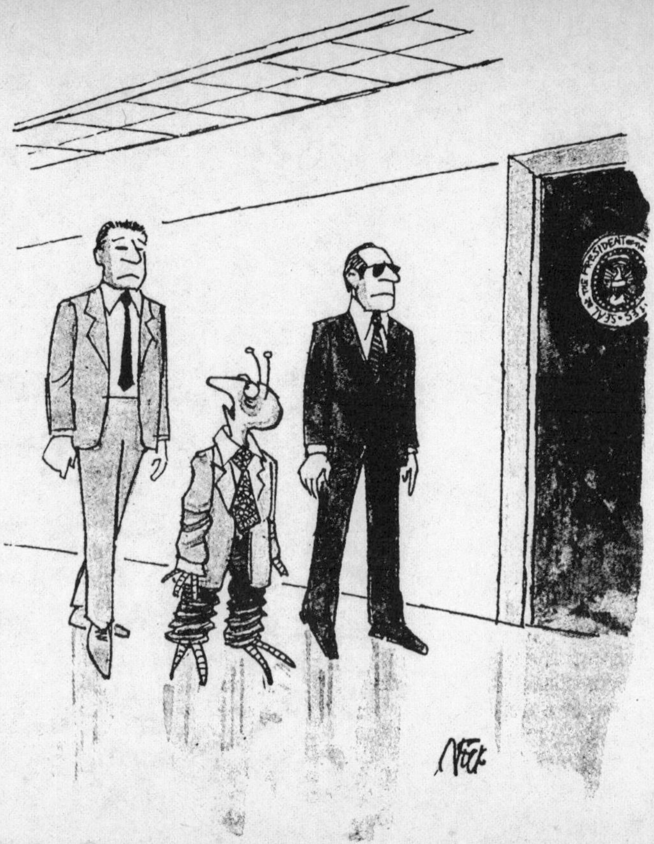

"President or no president, I feel pretty ridiculous in this get-up."

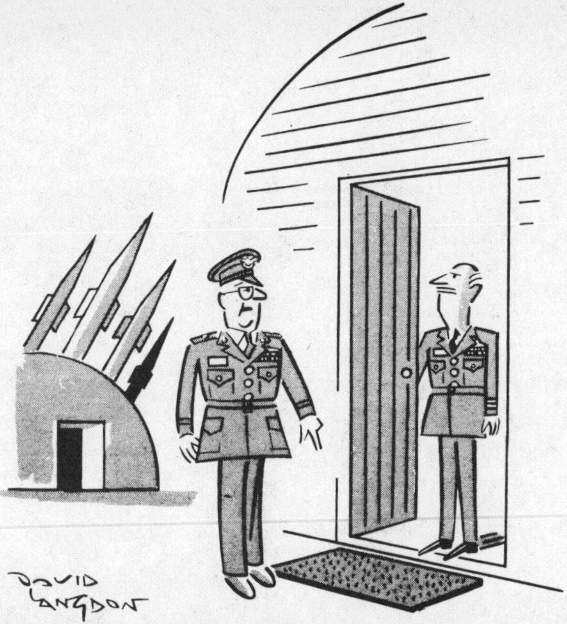

"The key's under the mat, okay?"

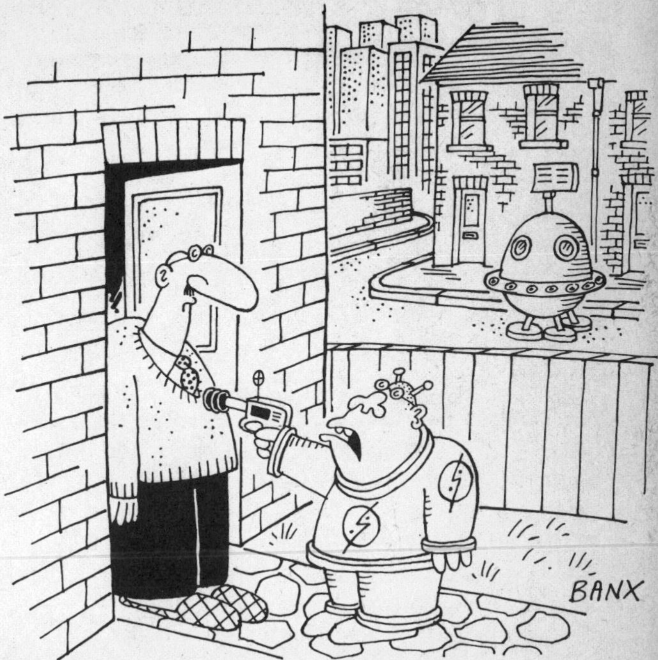

"You were tried and convicted in your absence, Earthman."

CHELM OF TRYG2 by Bill Tidy

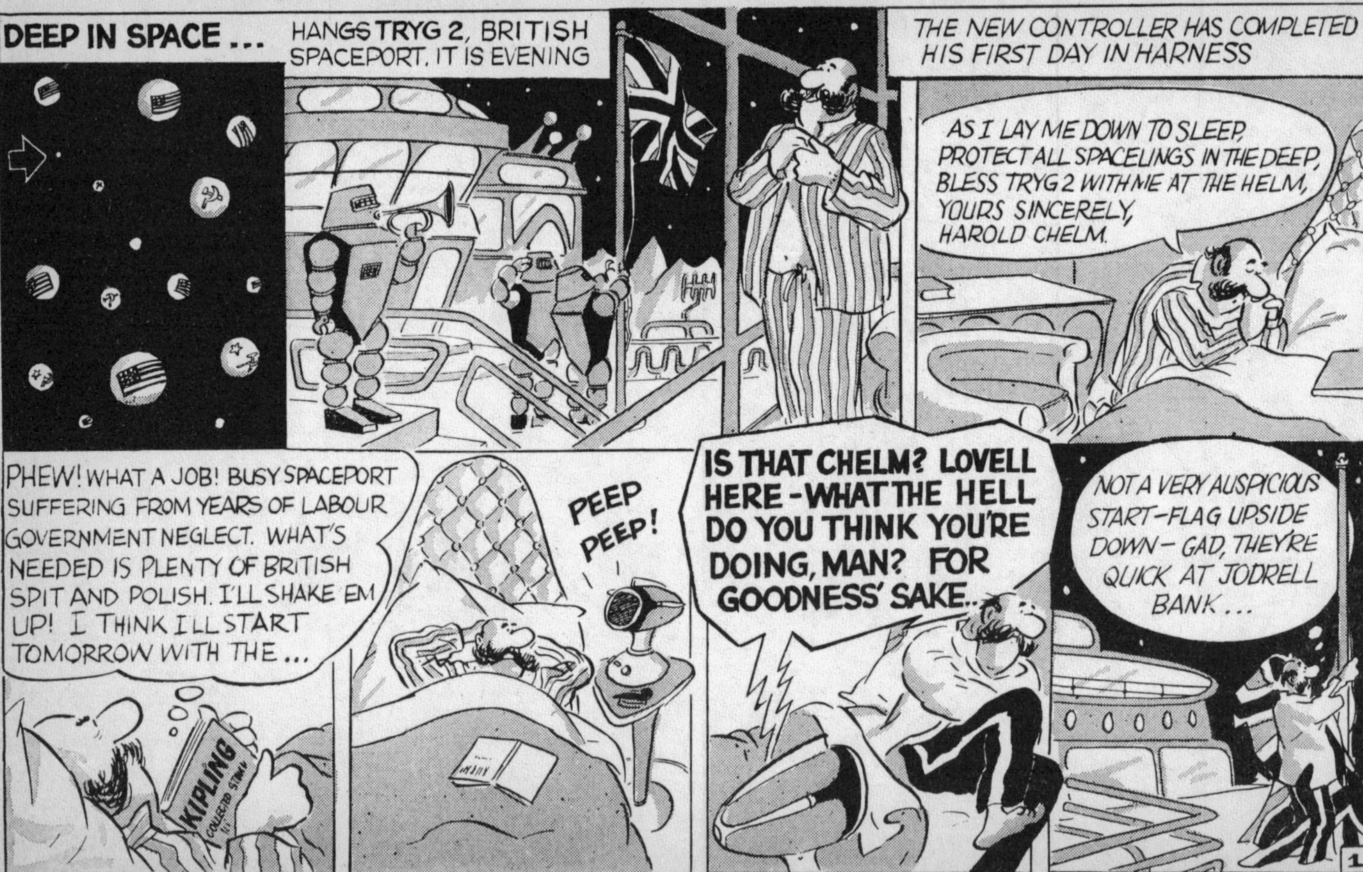

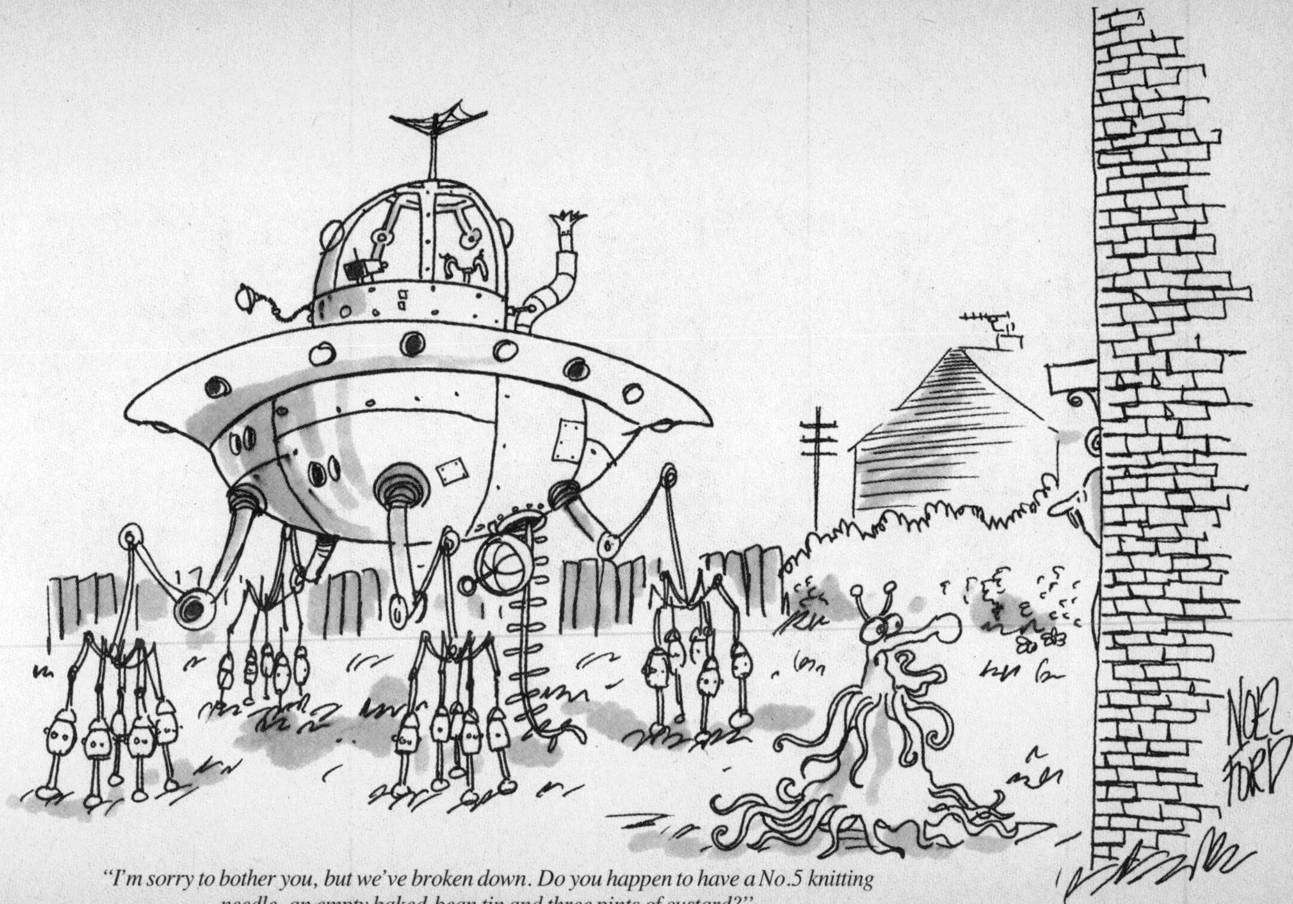

"I'm sorry to bother you, but we've broken down. Do you happen to have a No.5 knitting needle, an empty baked-bean tin and three pints of custard?"

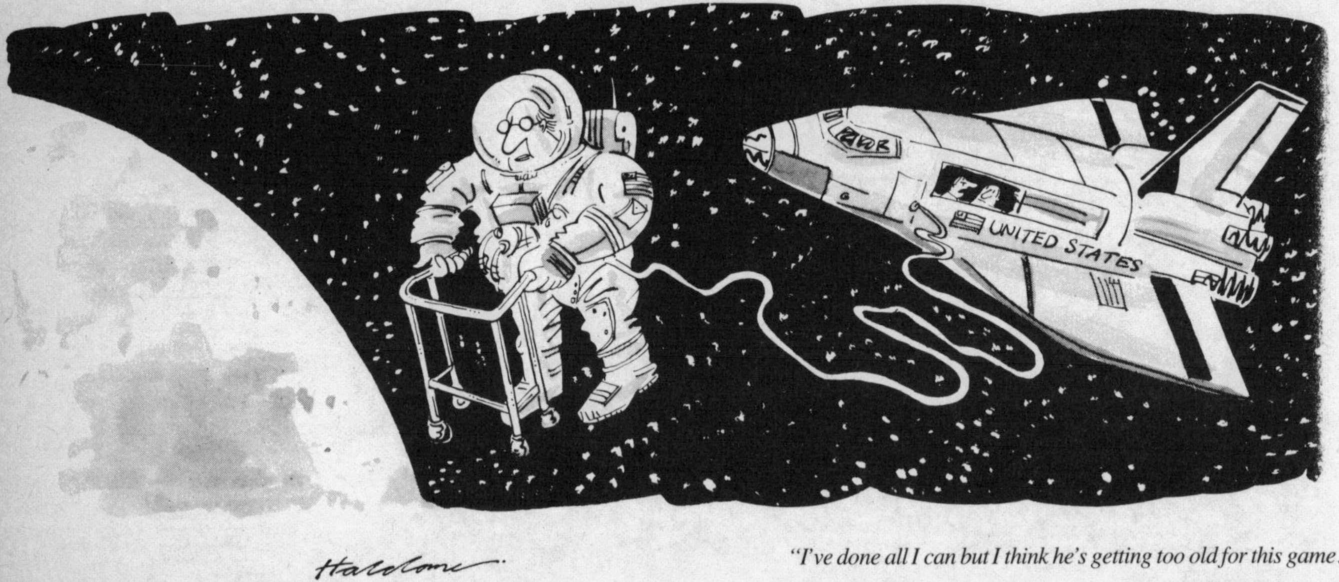

"I've done all I can but I think he's getting too old for this game."

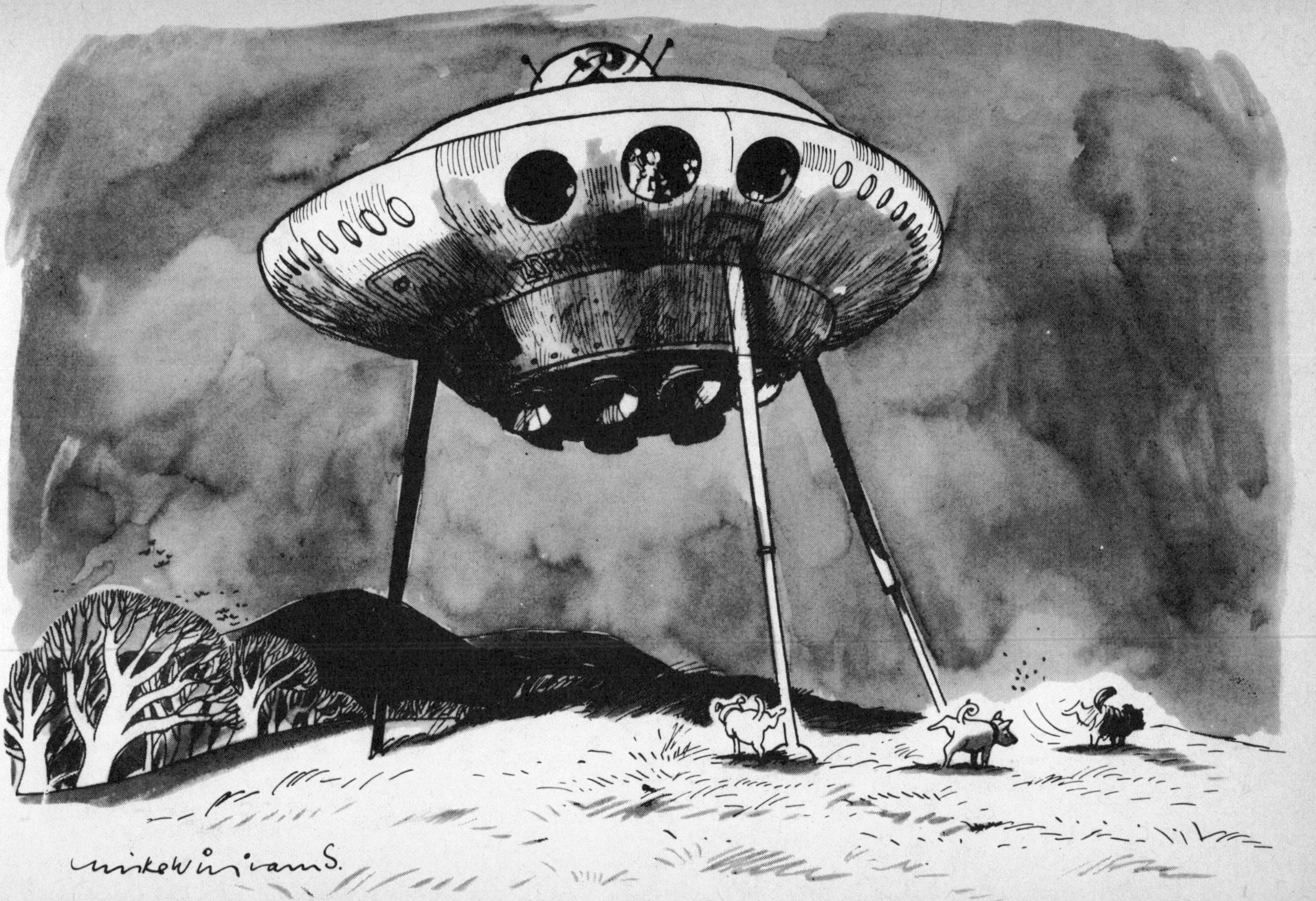

"Earthlings are now attacking our landing supports... repeat... Earthlings are now..."

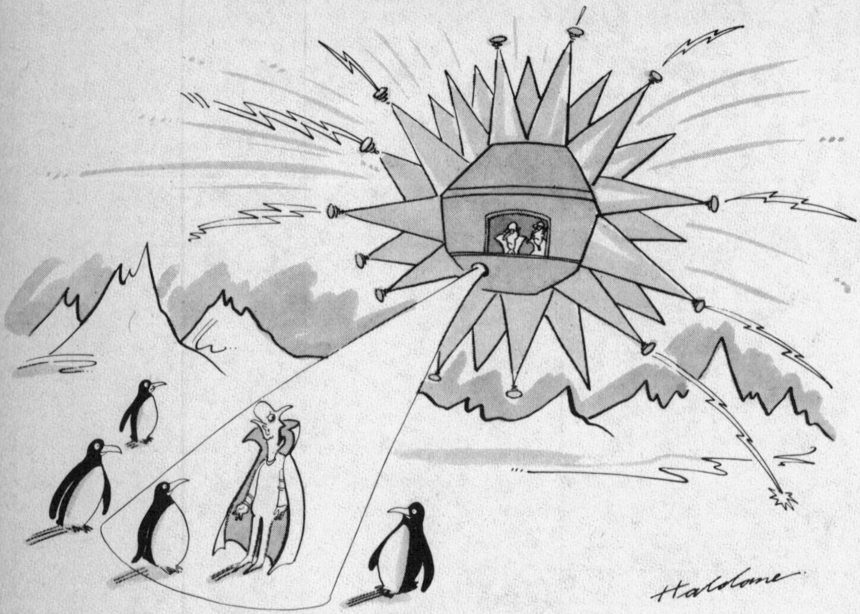

"I offer them the secrets of the universe and all they want to know is how to grill fish."

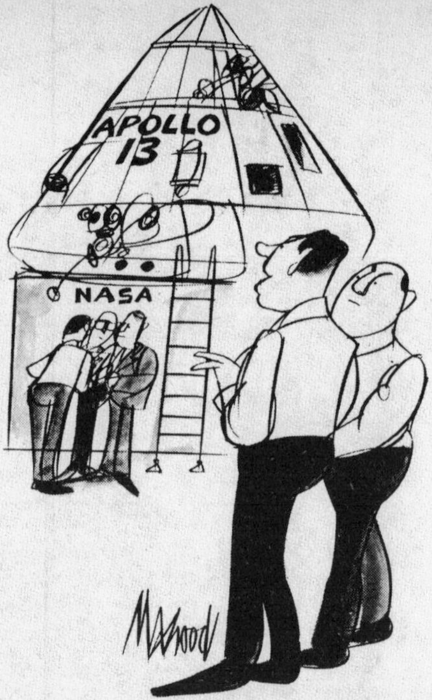

"What's all the fuss about? After all, it got them there and brought them back."

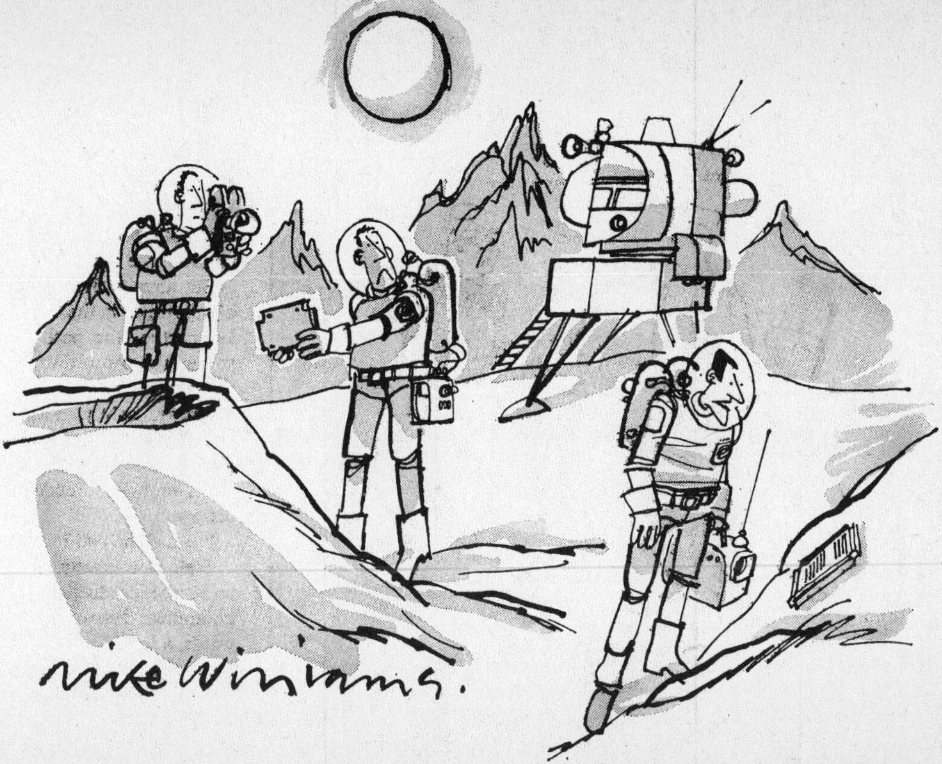

"Hey, there's another plaque here! It says 'We came in peace for the benefit of all Venusians. Trespassers will be annihilated.'"

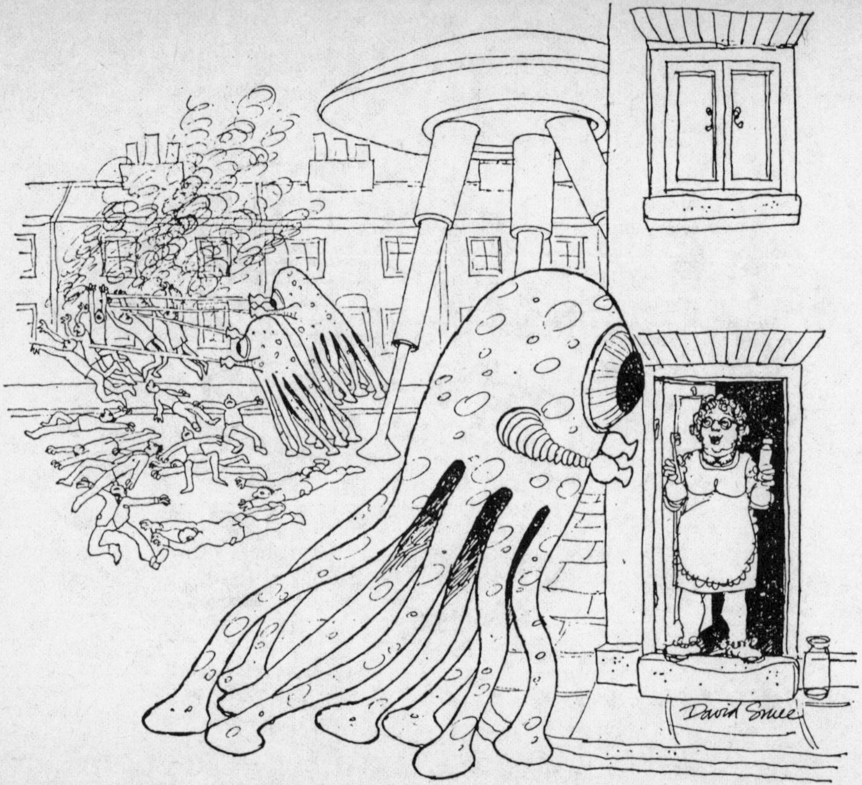

"You are Tommy Tooth Decay and I claim the 'Dentaglo' £5 bonus!"

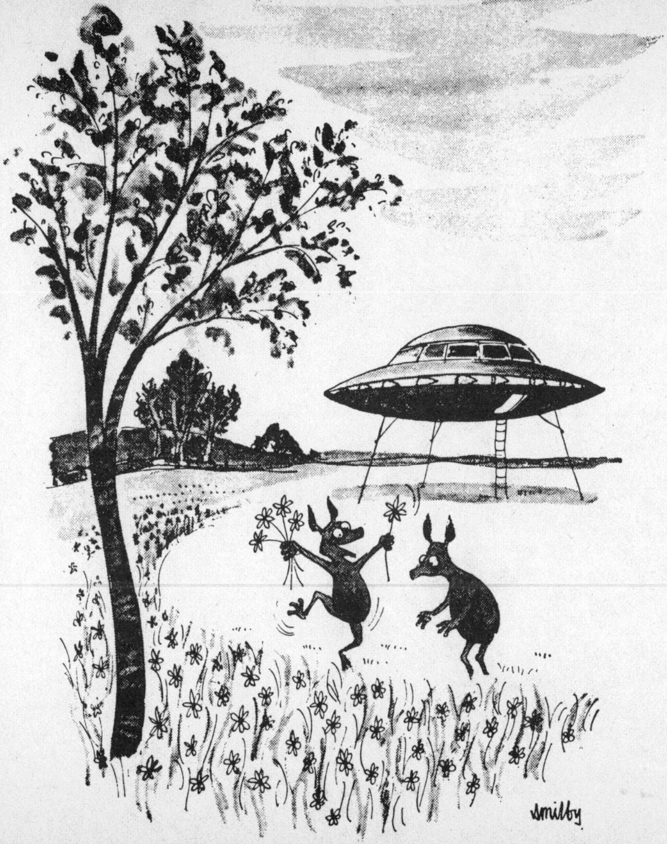

"Gold – it's gold."

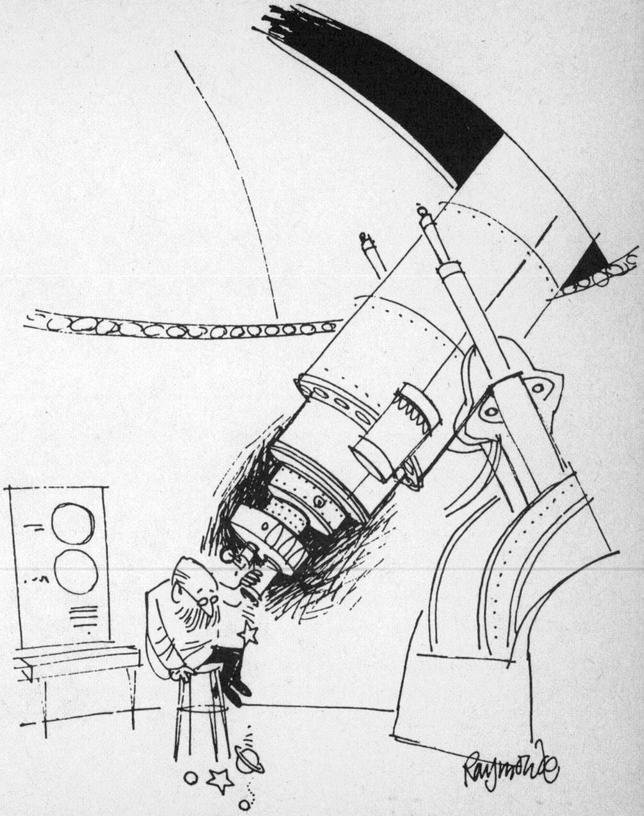

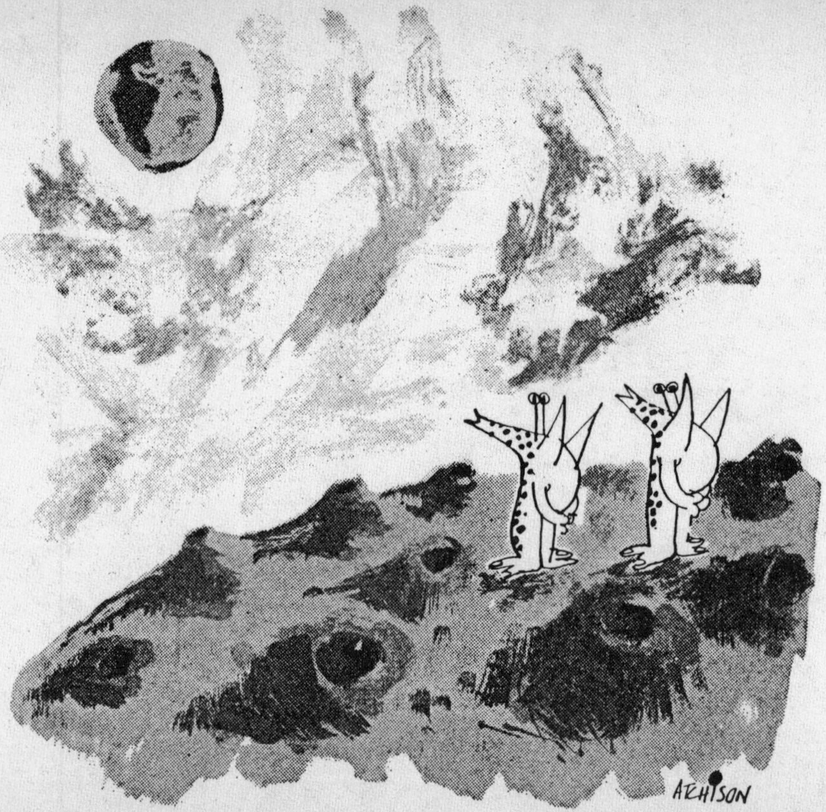

"Whichever gets here first, I suppose we'll have to look out for our women!"

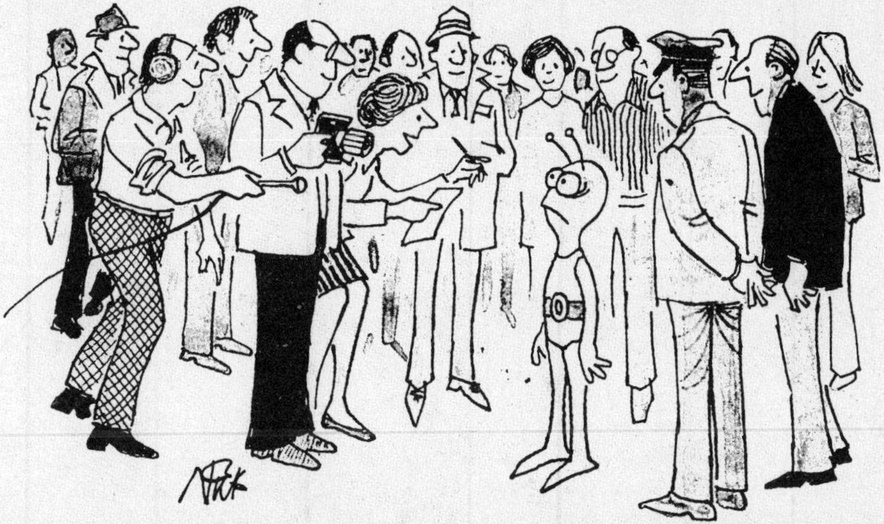

"'Woman's World' magazine, sir – would you describe yourself as Eau-de-Nil or Spring Fern?"

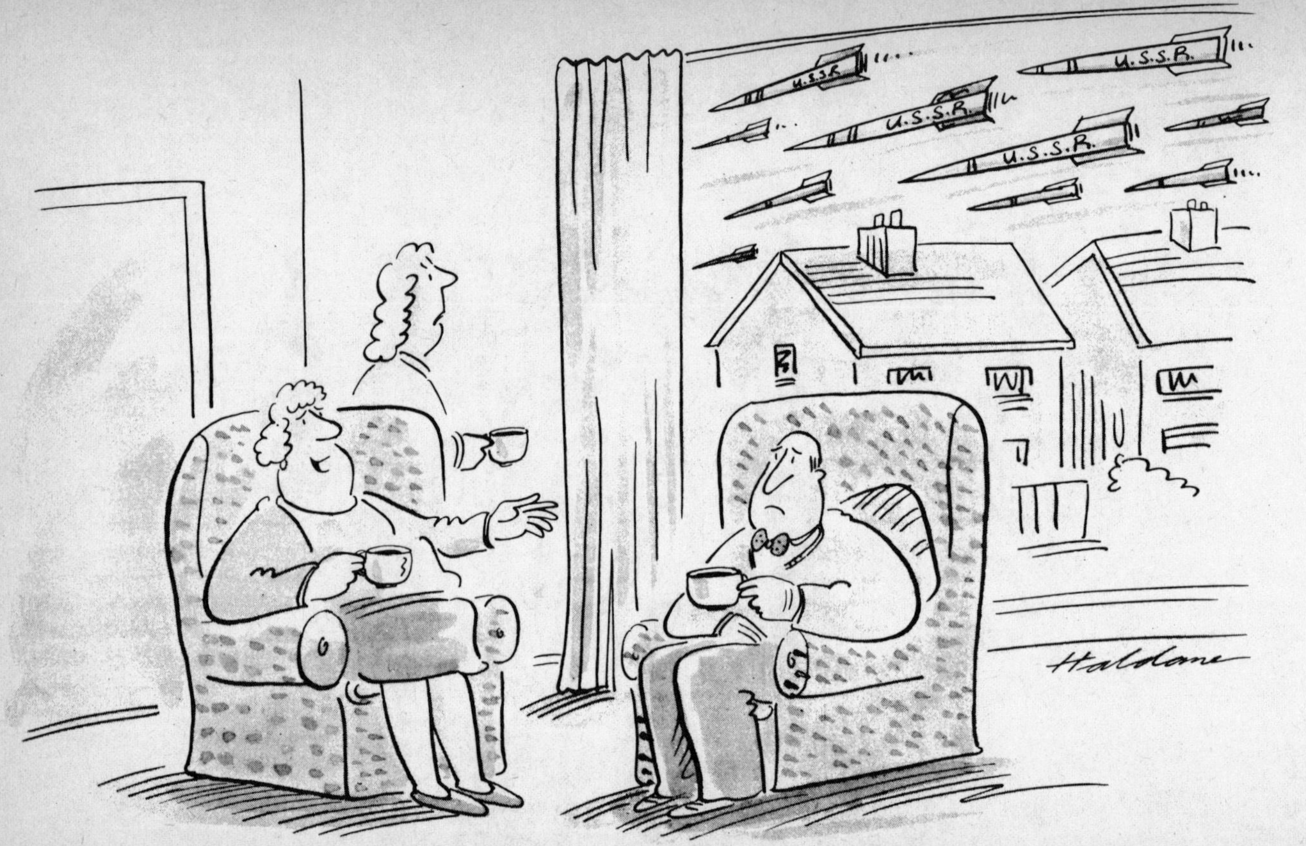

"Normally Roger wouldn't touch instant coffee."

CHELM OF TRYG 2 by Bill Tidy

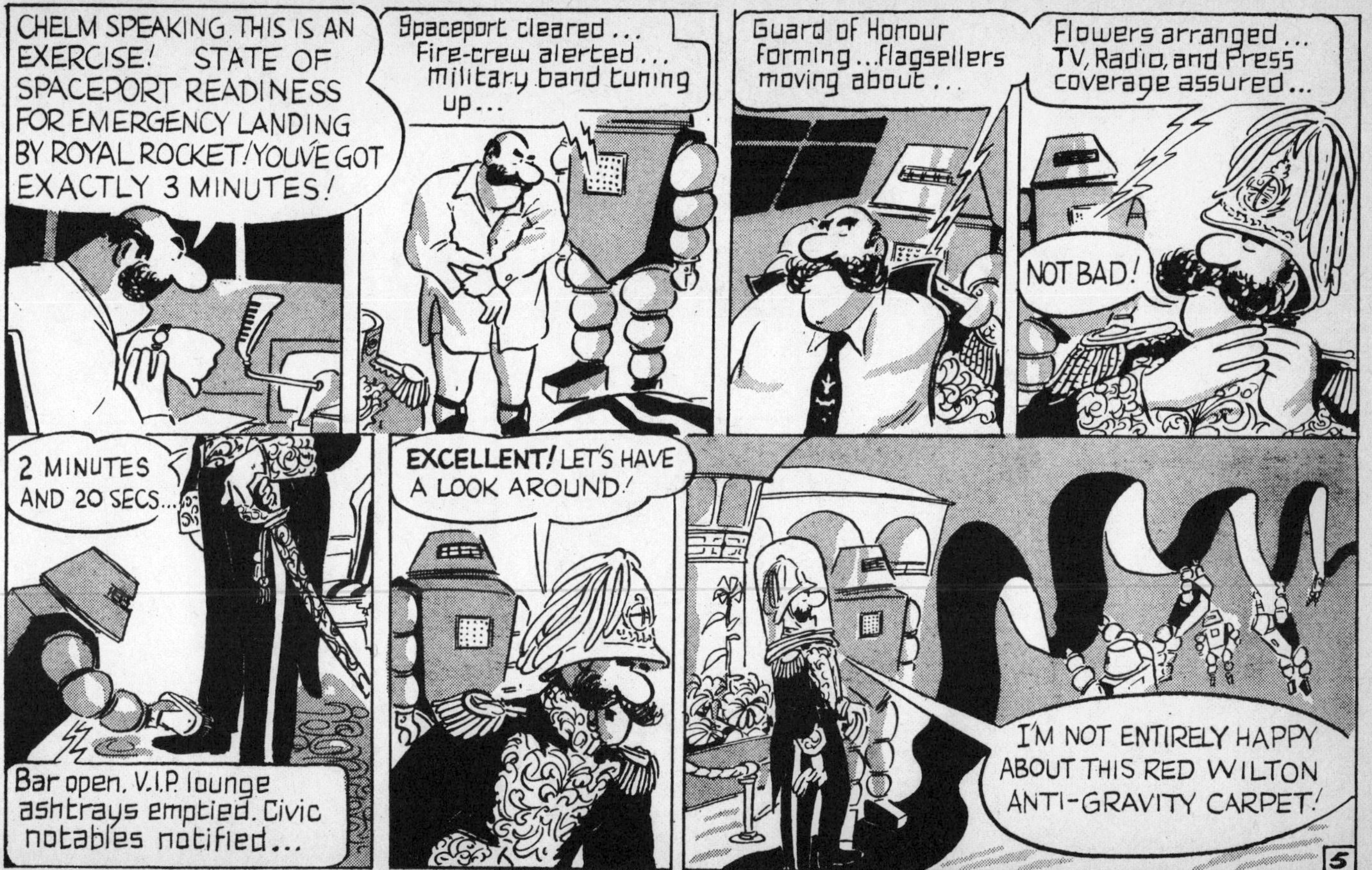

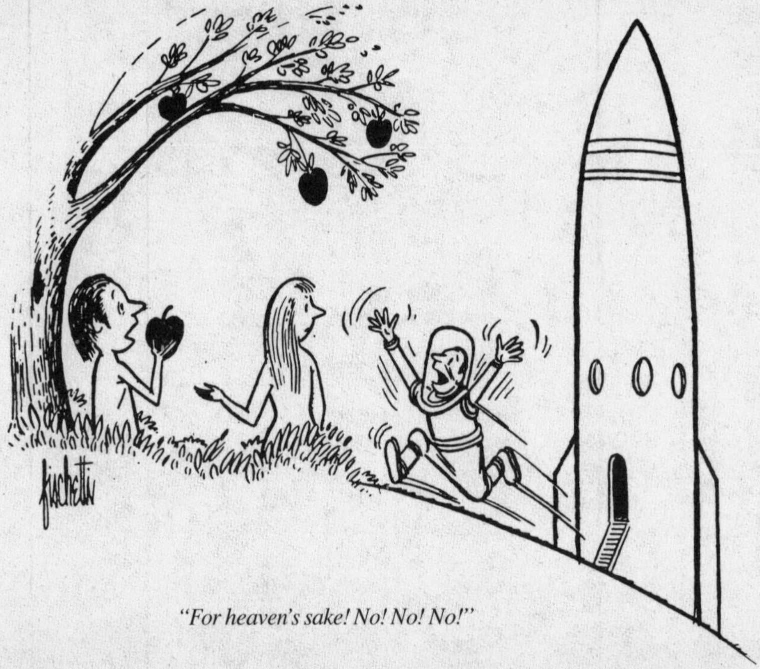

"For heaven's sake! No! No! No!"

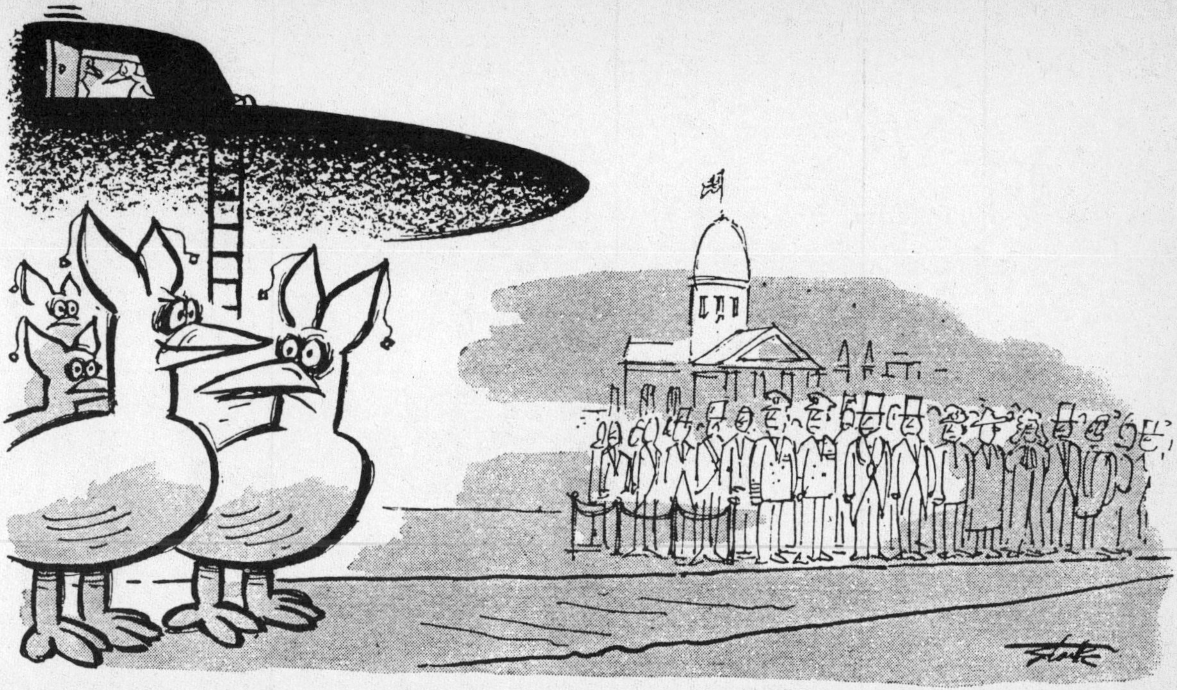

"Now, for goodness sake try to keep a straight face – remember we are ambassadors of our planet."

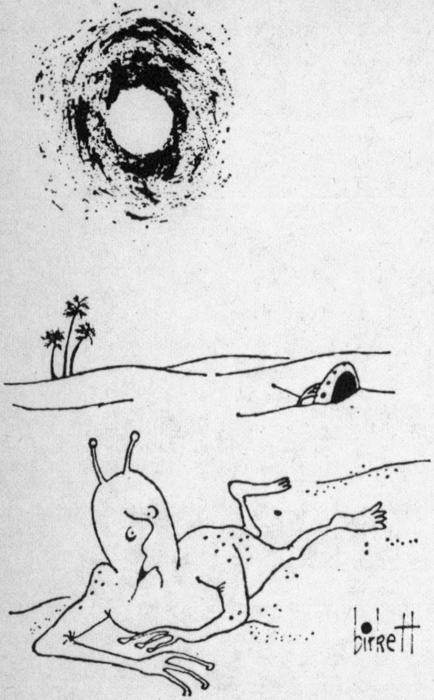

"Ammonia! Ammonia!"

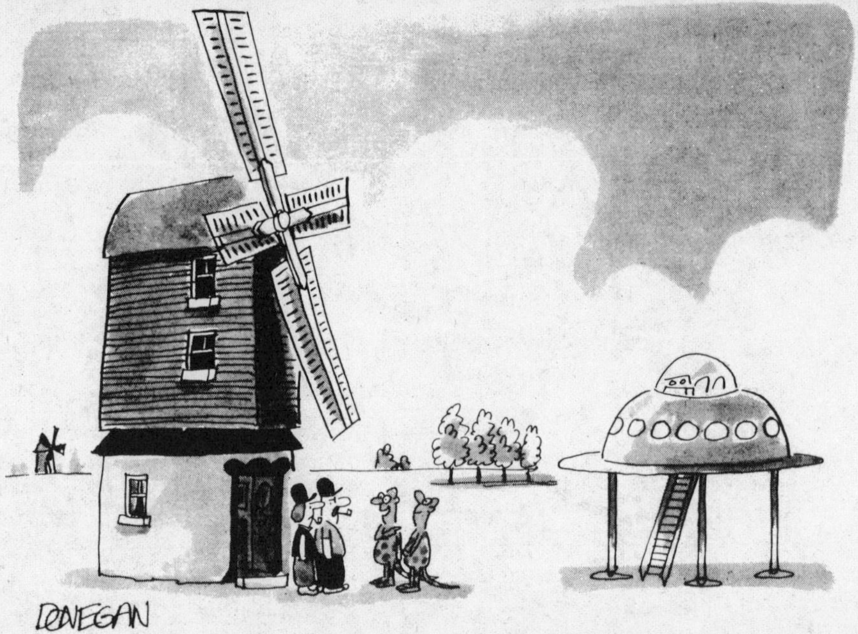

"You have a go in ours, and we'll have a go in yours, okay?"

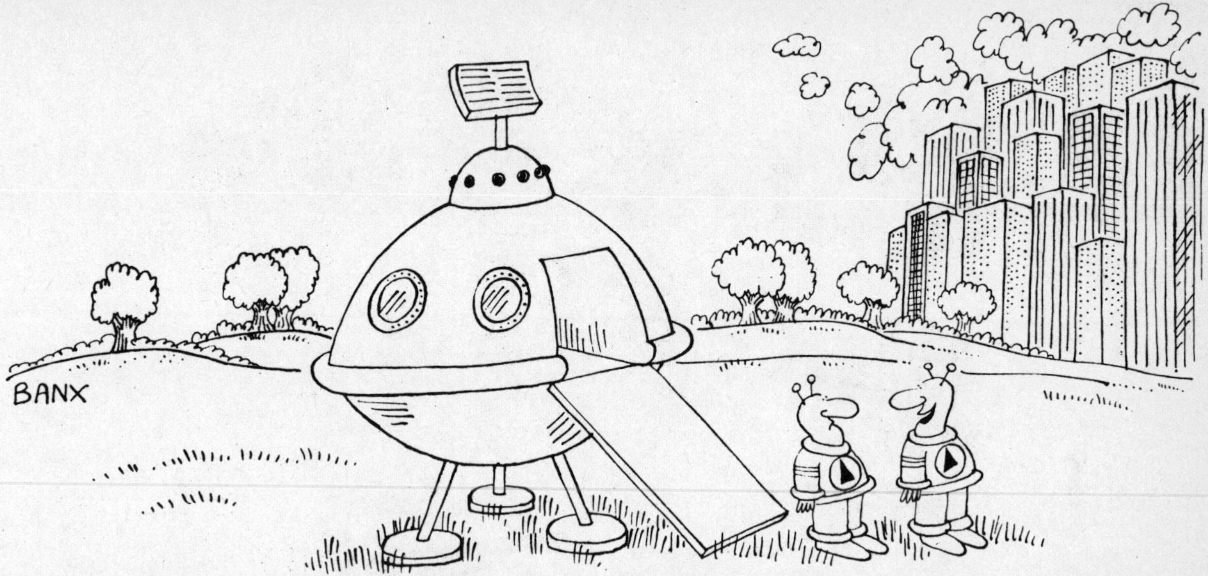

"This is the bit I like best – flaunting their rabies laws."

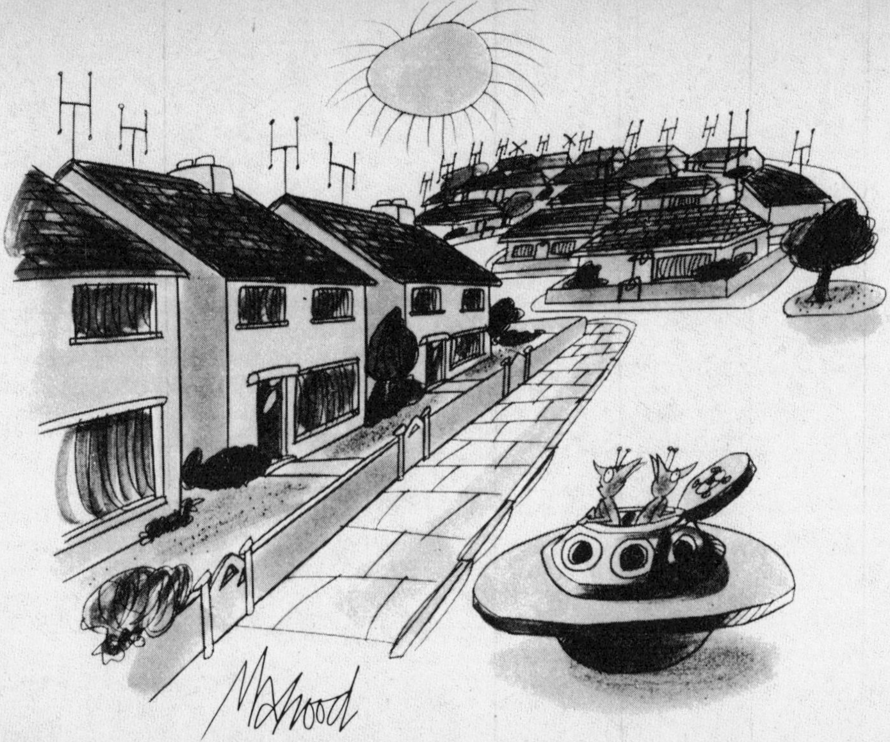

"Agreed, then – no sign of intelligent life on Earth?"

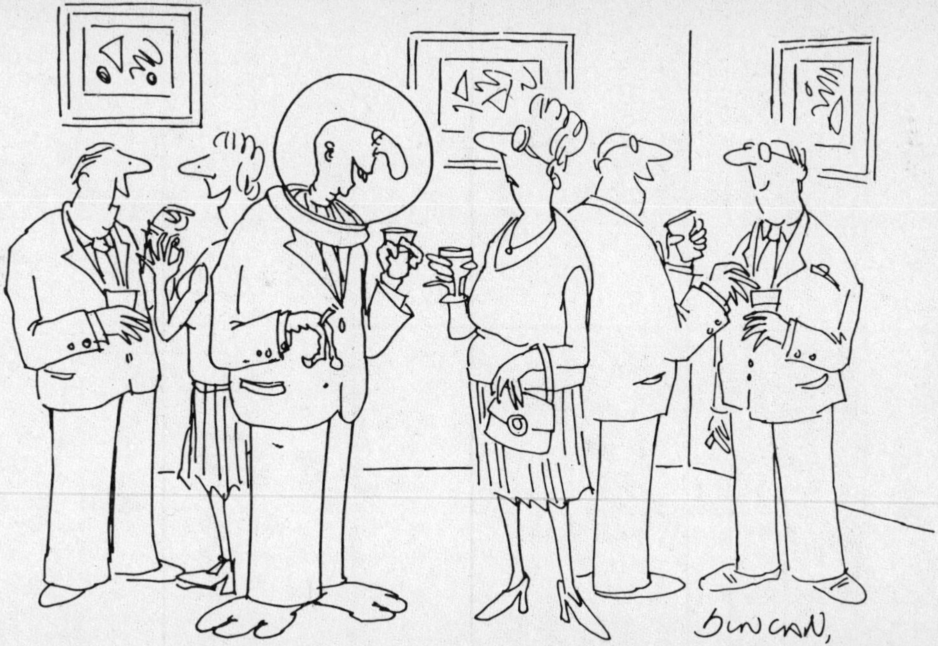

" 'Good heavens, we don't all sport antennae, you know.' "

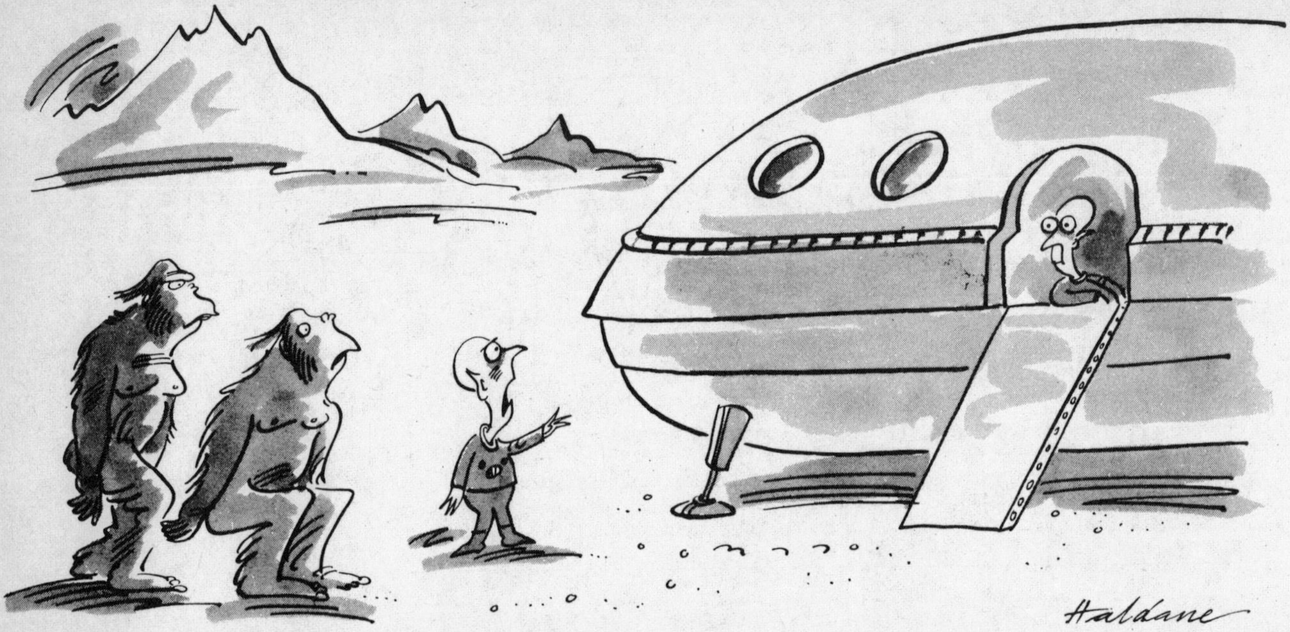

"All they want is the secret of fire, so we're still stuck with 52,000,000 digital watches."

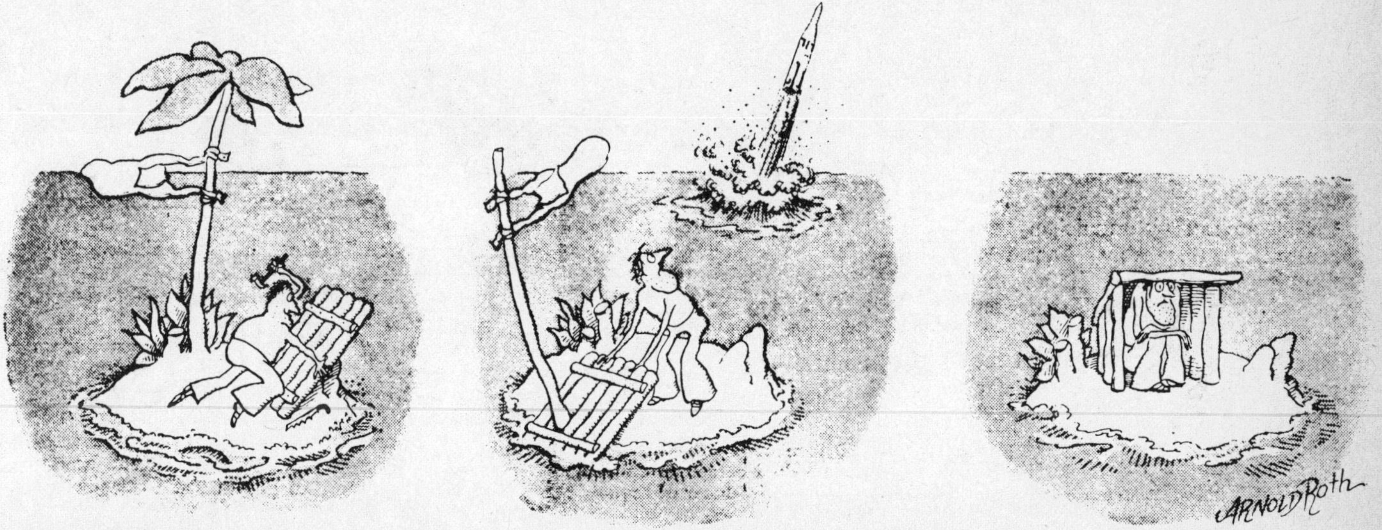
ARNOLD Roth

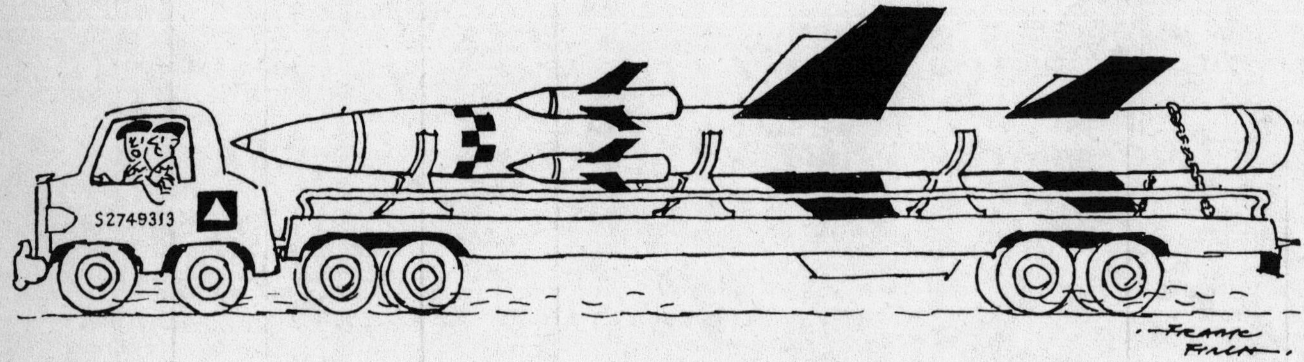

"Do you have to say 'Venus here we come!' every time we hit a bump?"

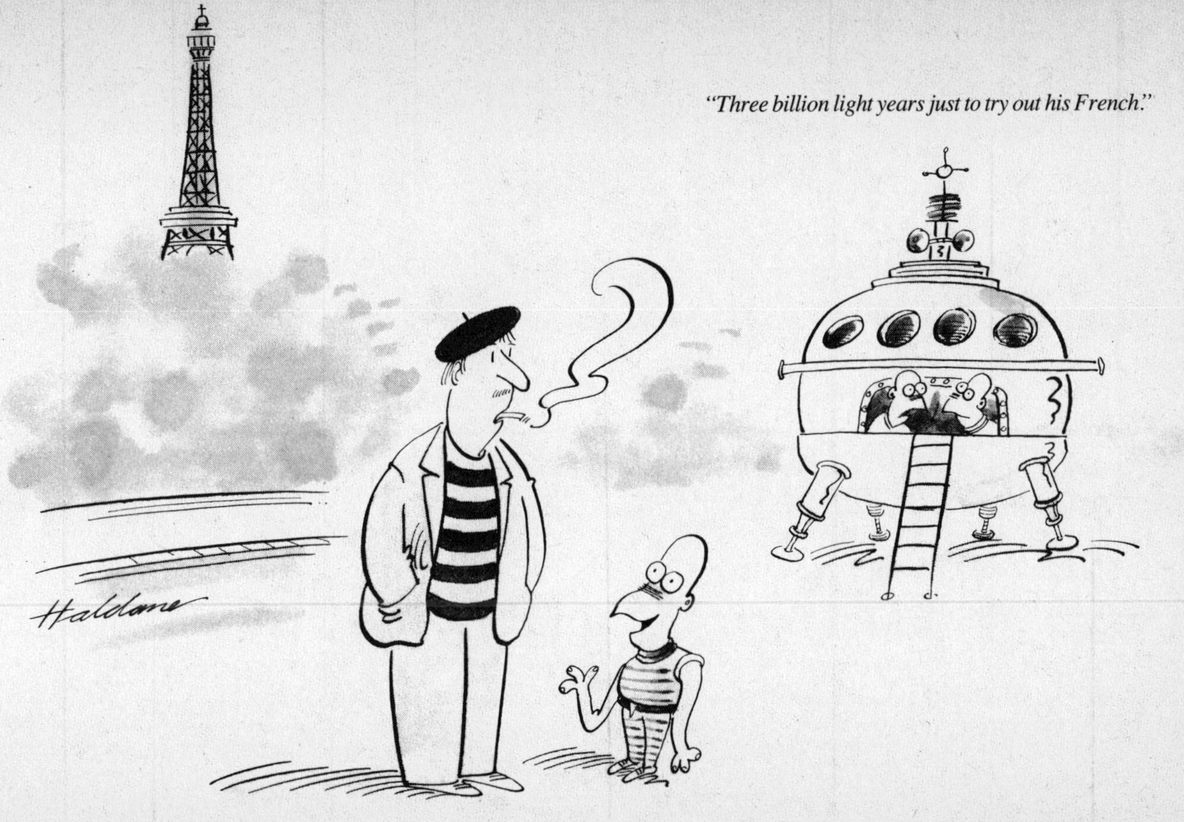

"Three billion light years just to try out his French."

CHELM OF TRYG 2 by Bill Tidy

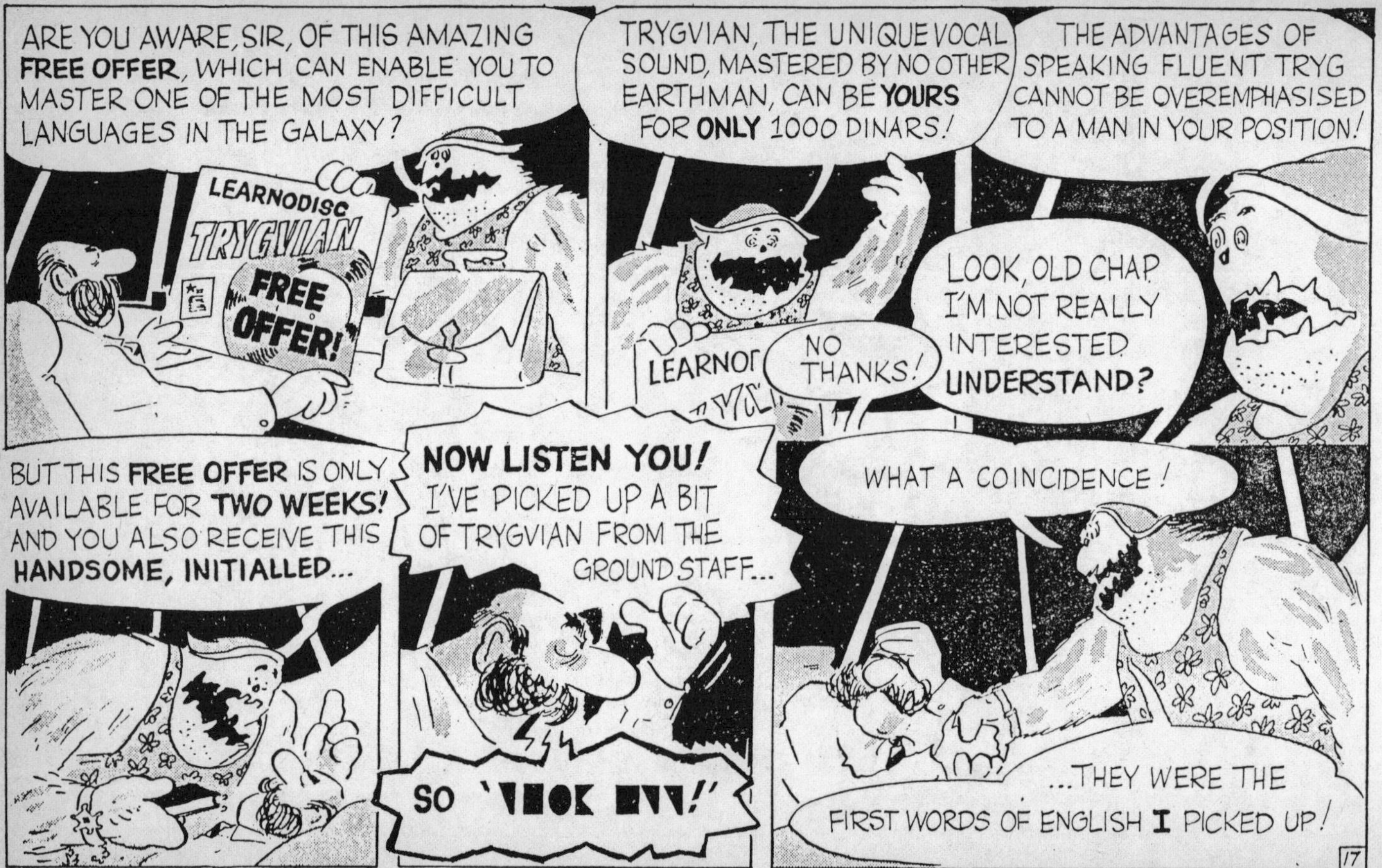

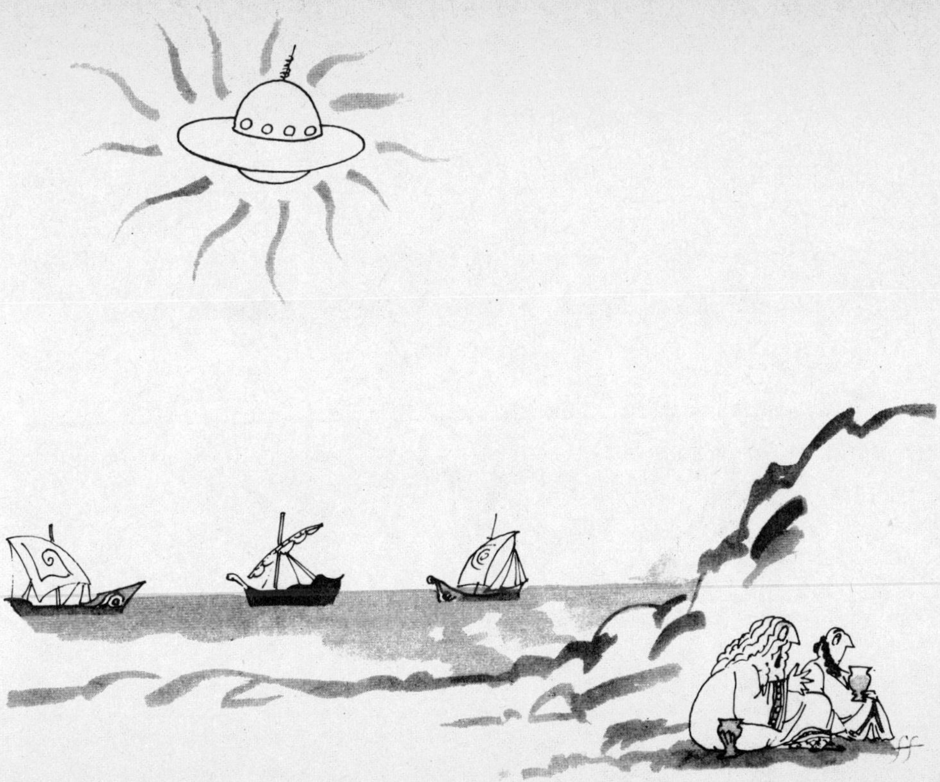

"I can get on with the Phoenicians, Greeks and Etruscans. It's the Martians."

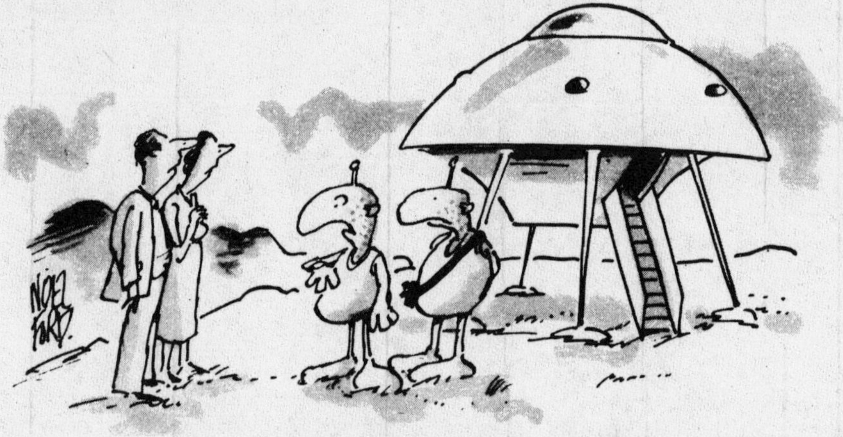

"Well, must dash, the tour itinerary gives us only 32.46 minutes for this solar system."

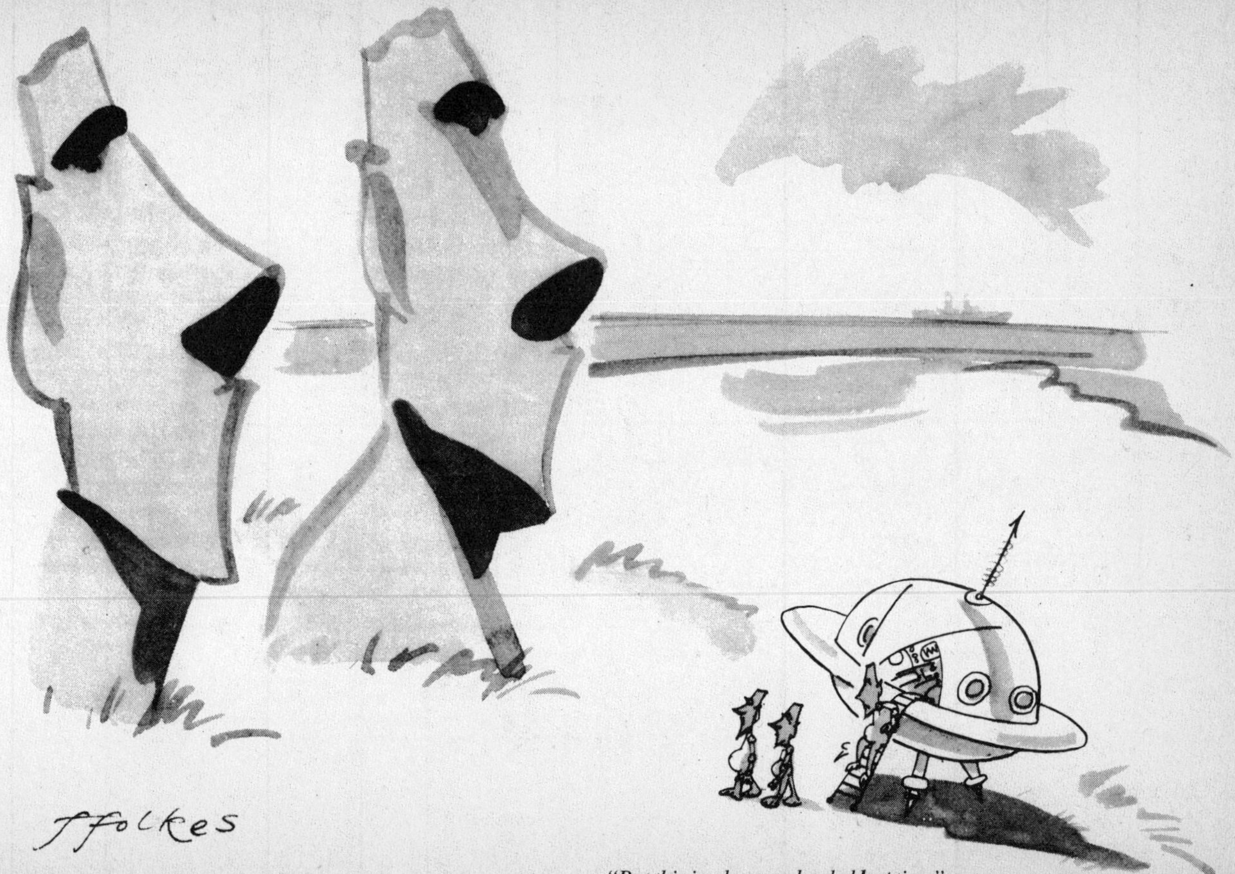

"But this is where we landed **last** time."

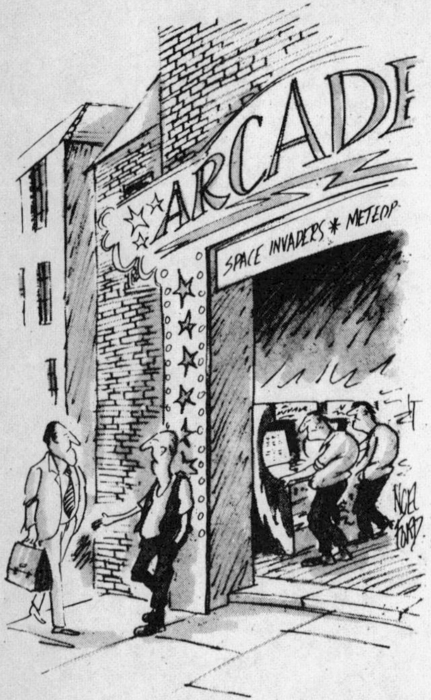

"Spare 20p to save planet earth, sir?"

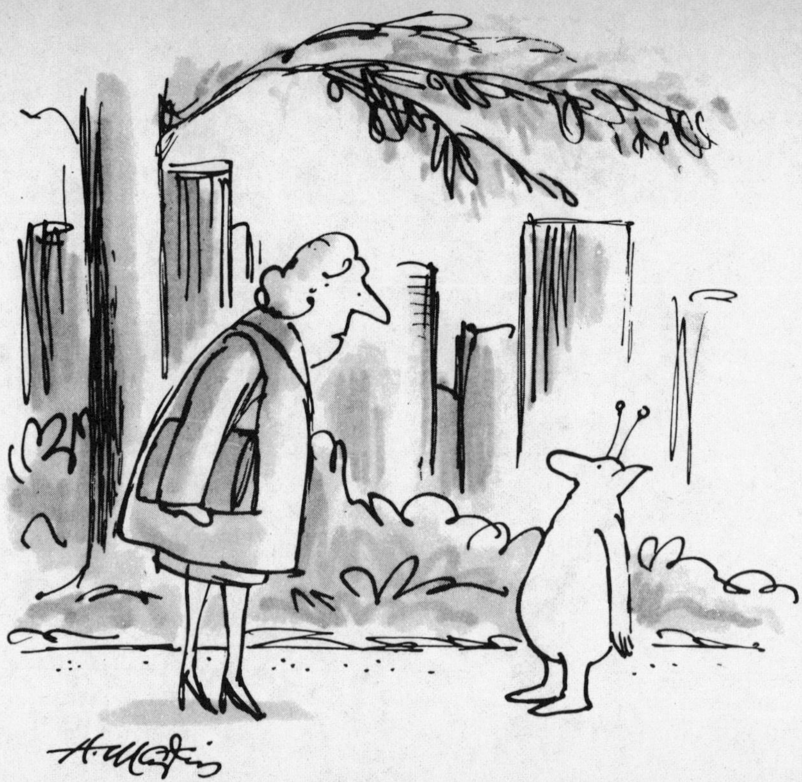

"I don't care what planet you're from, you can't run around earth stark naked!"

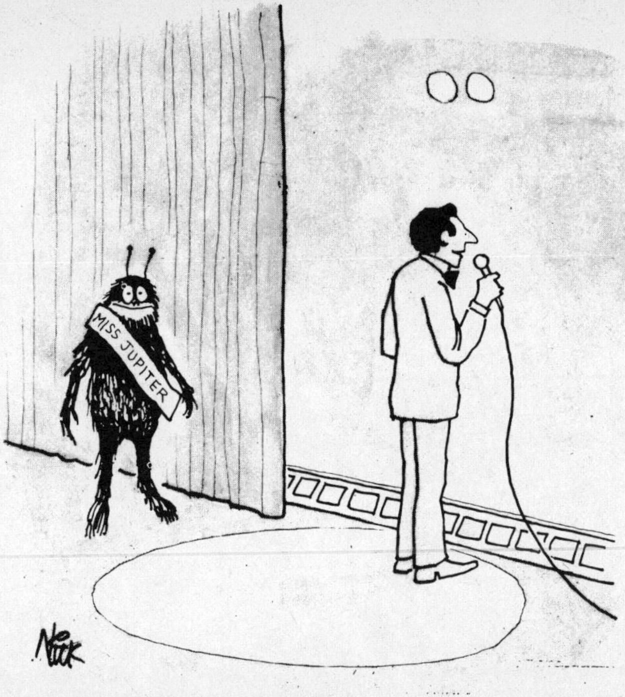

". . . and the next contestant hoping to become Miss Universe . . ."

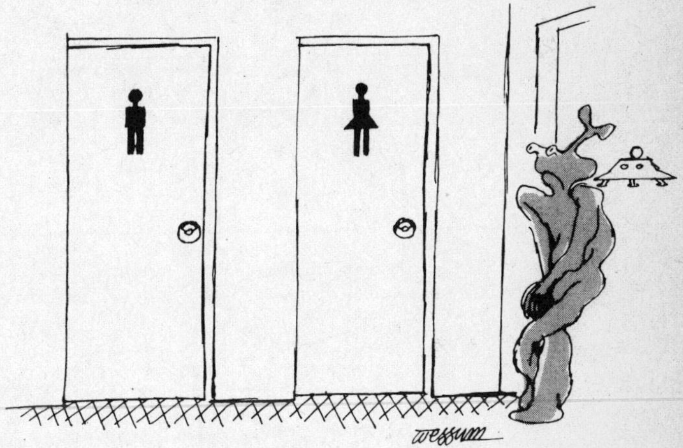

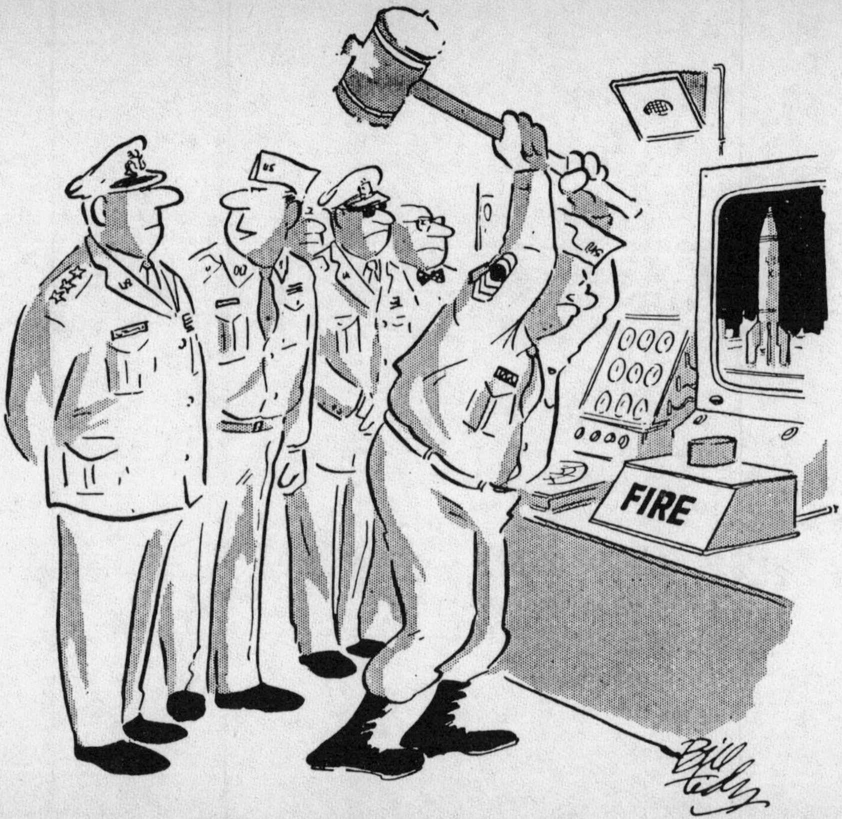

"This is gonna be the highest yet, General."

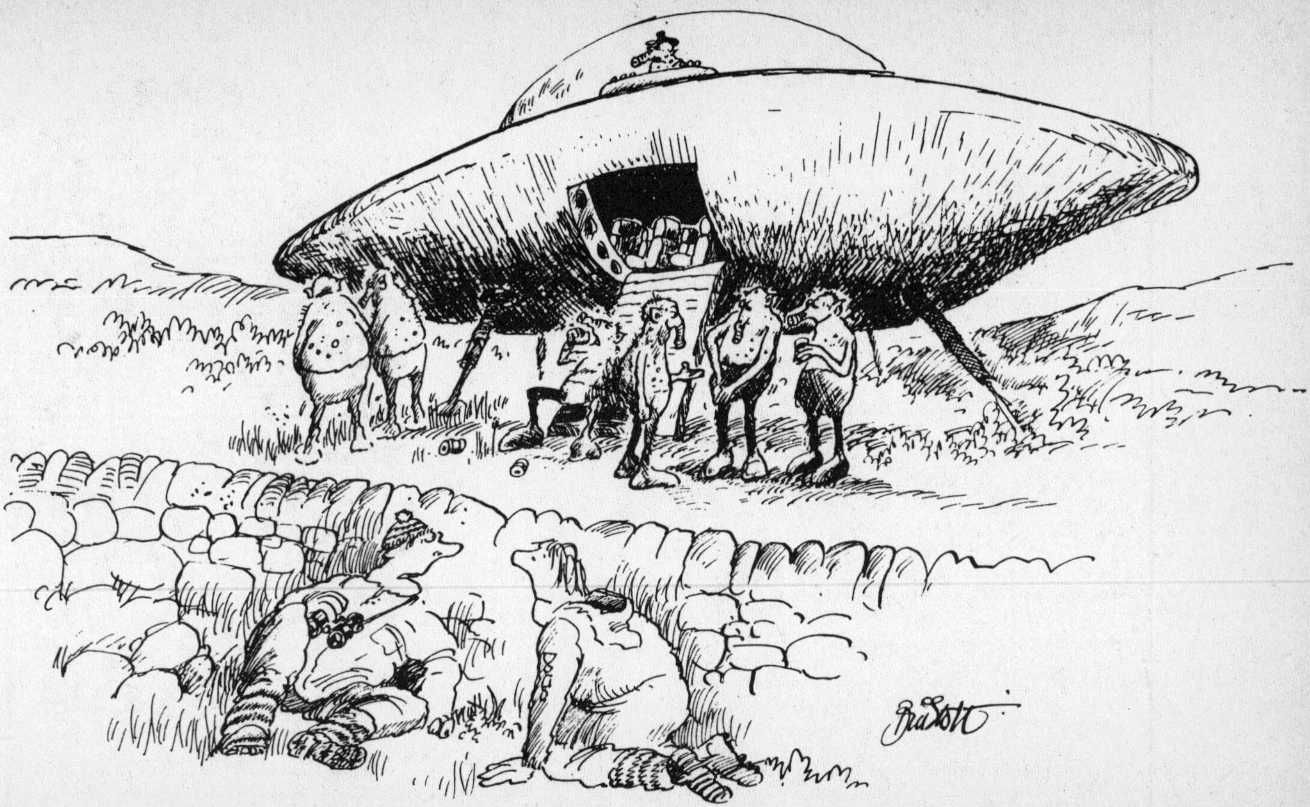

"They appear to be having a whip-round for the driver!"

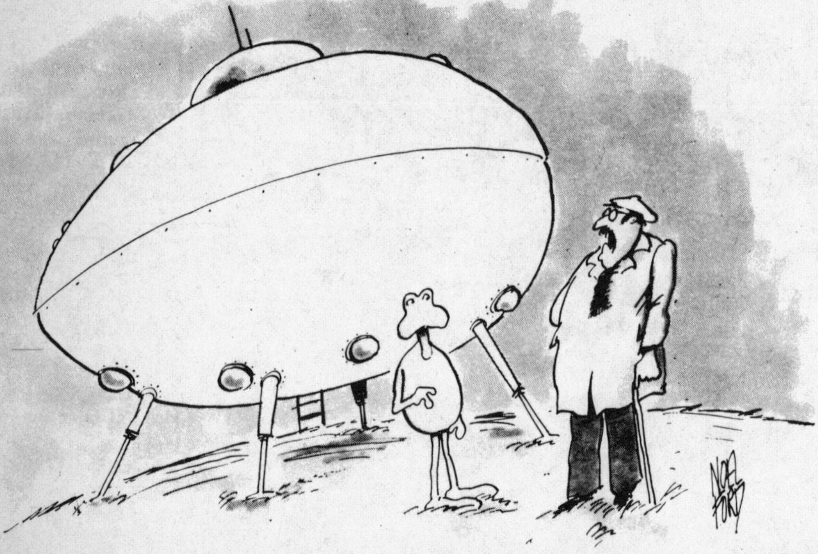

*"And how much has **that** bloody thing cost the ratepayers?"*

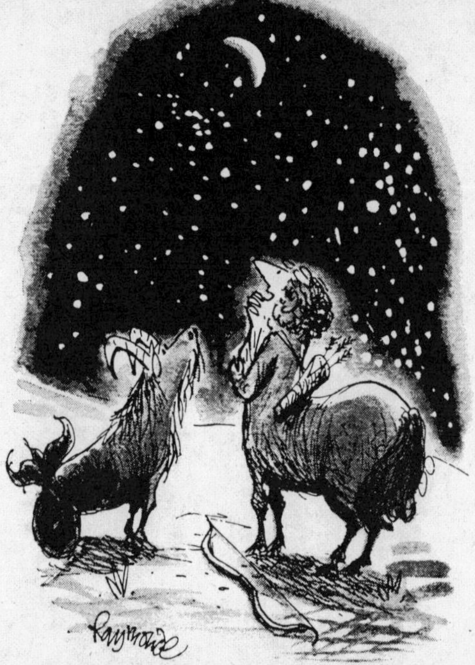

"D'you think there's anything in this astrology business?"

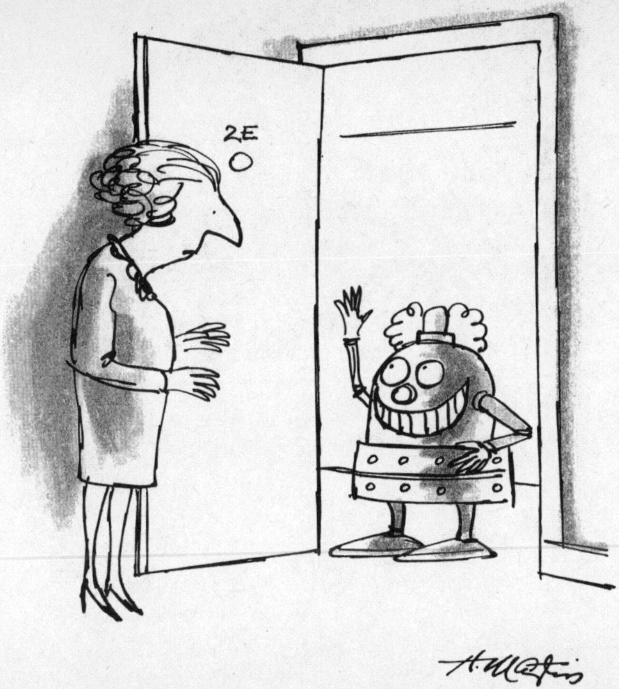

"Hi! I'm BU-4-DEx and it's like I'm right out of some movie."

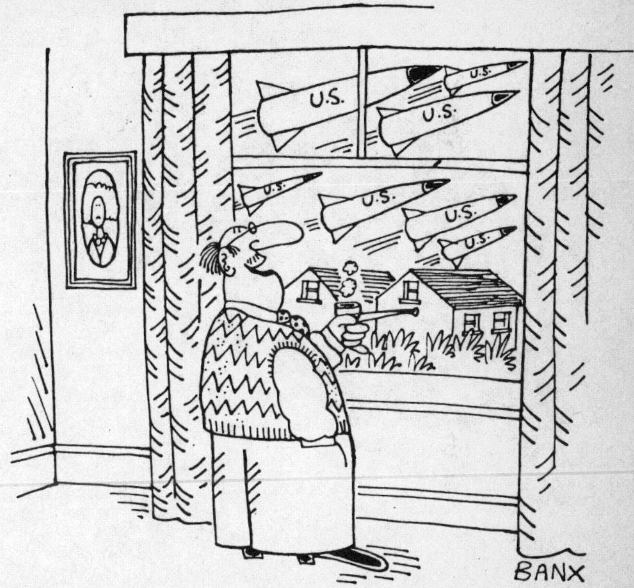

"It's all right, Sophie, here come **ours** *now."*

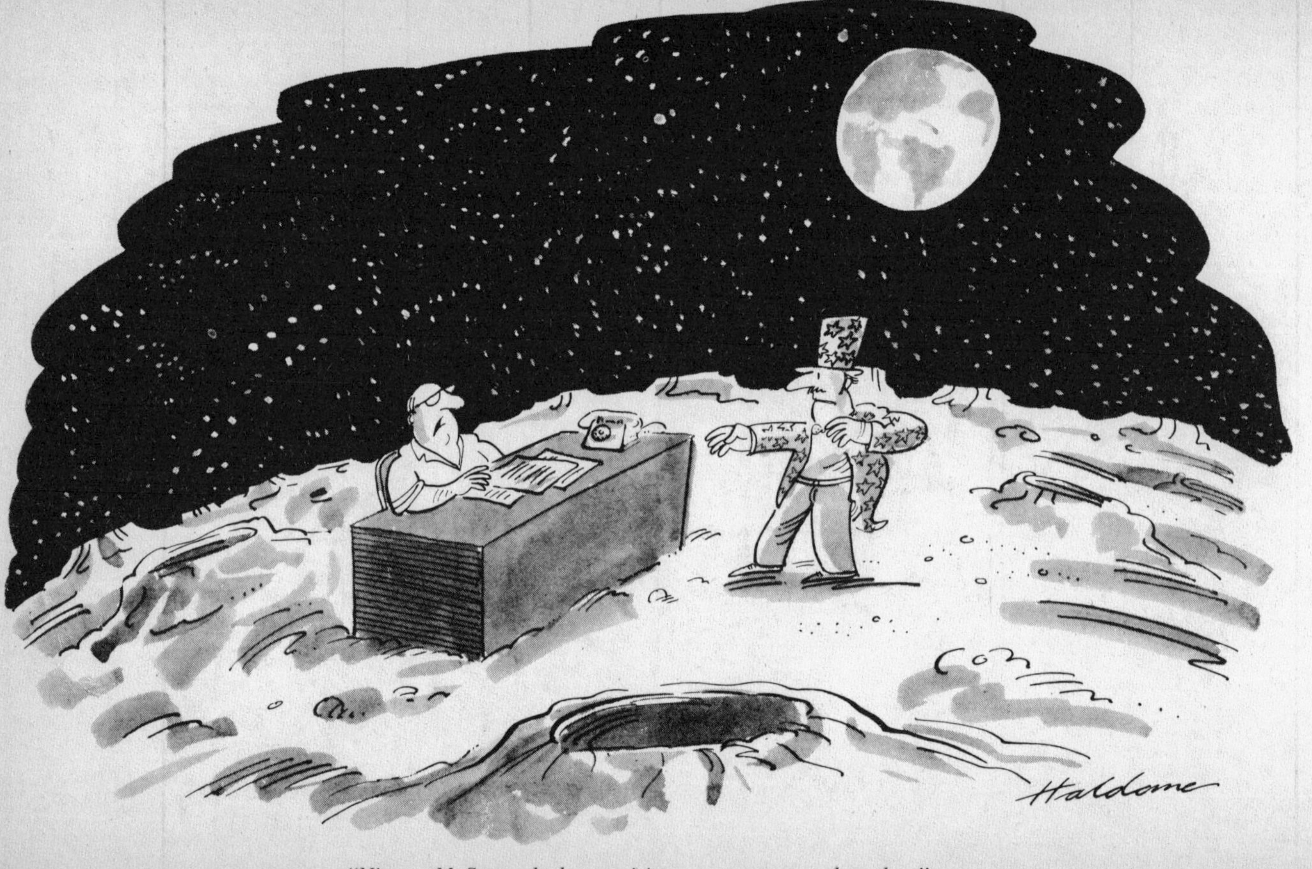

"Nice try, Mr Stupendo, but magicians are ten-a-penny these days."

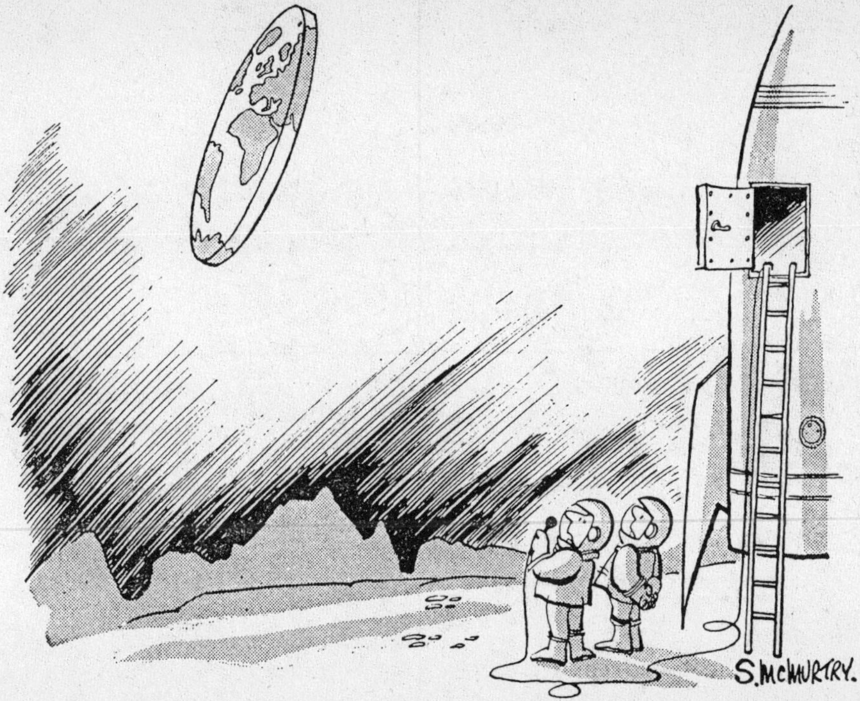

"Hello earth... look, I'm not quite certain how to put this..."

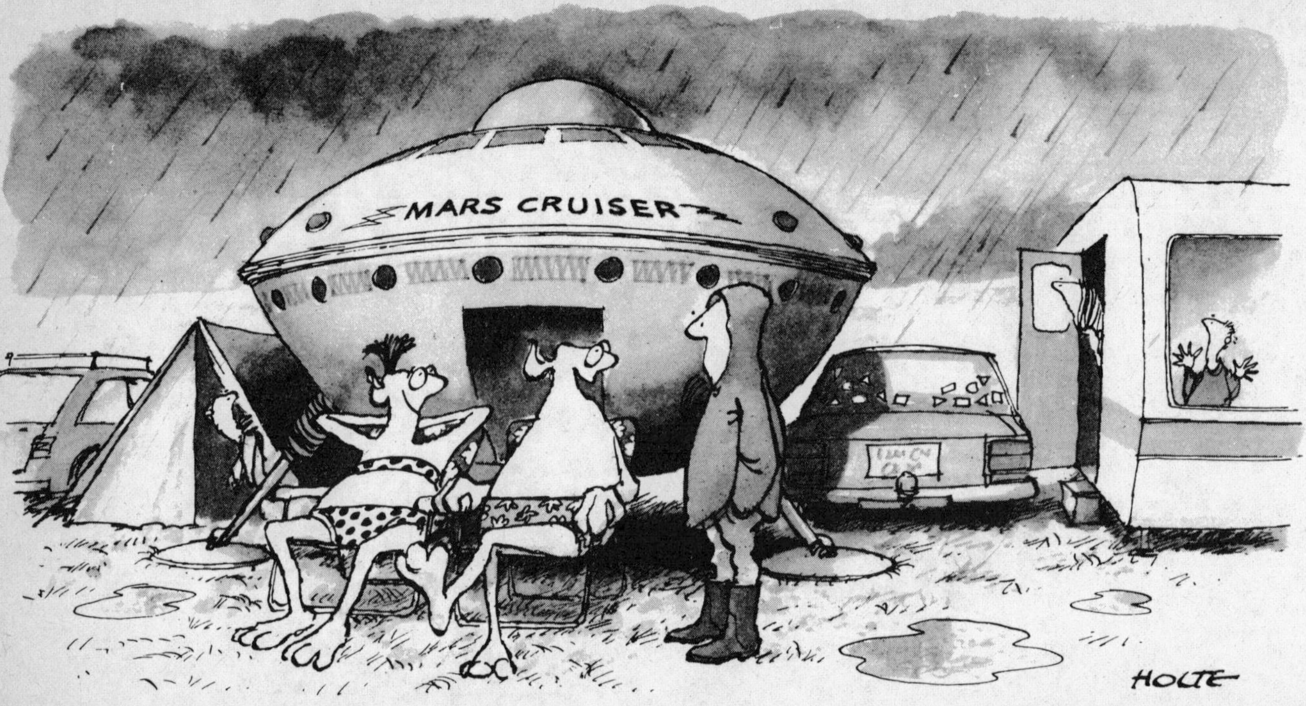

"It's a damn sight better than the weather we've been having lately, I can tell you."

CHELM OF TRYG 2, British Space Station of the Future by Bill Tidy

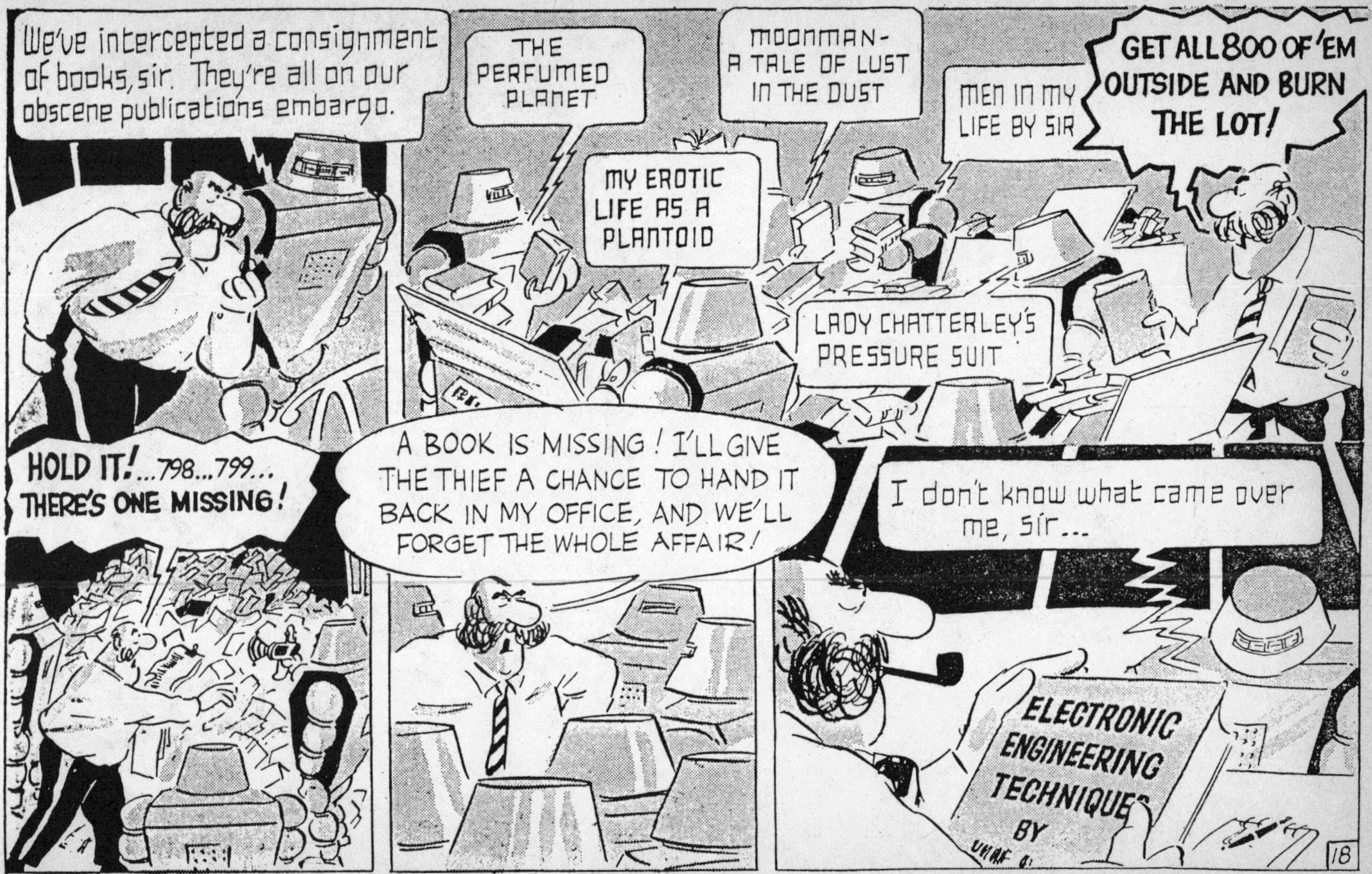

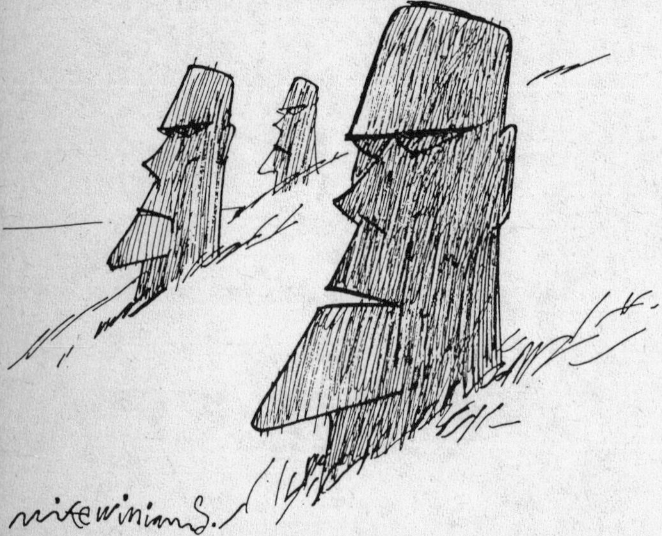

"Sunshine or not I'll be damn'd glad when this observation stint's over and we can get back to Mars."

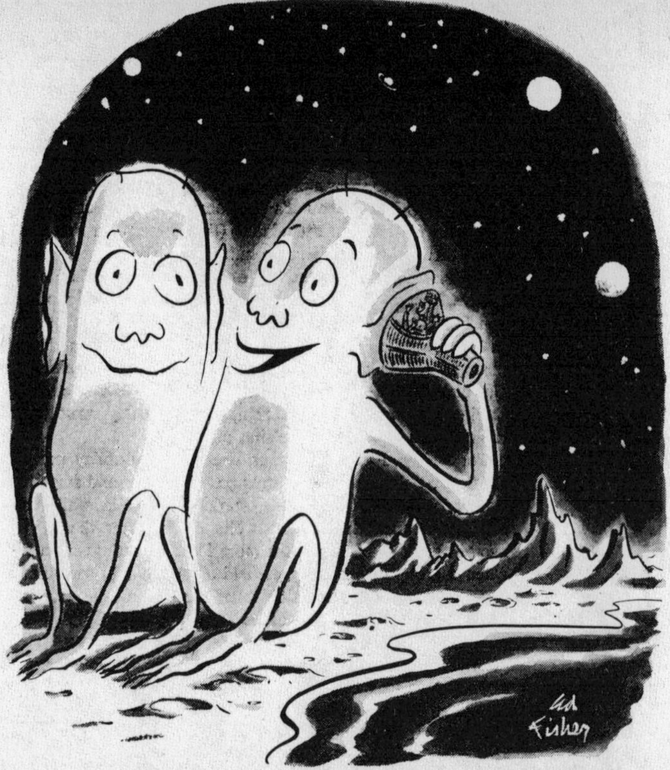

"Listen! – the sound of the roaring of the depths!"

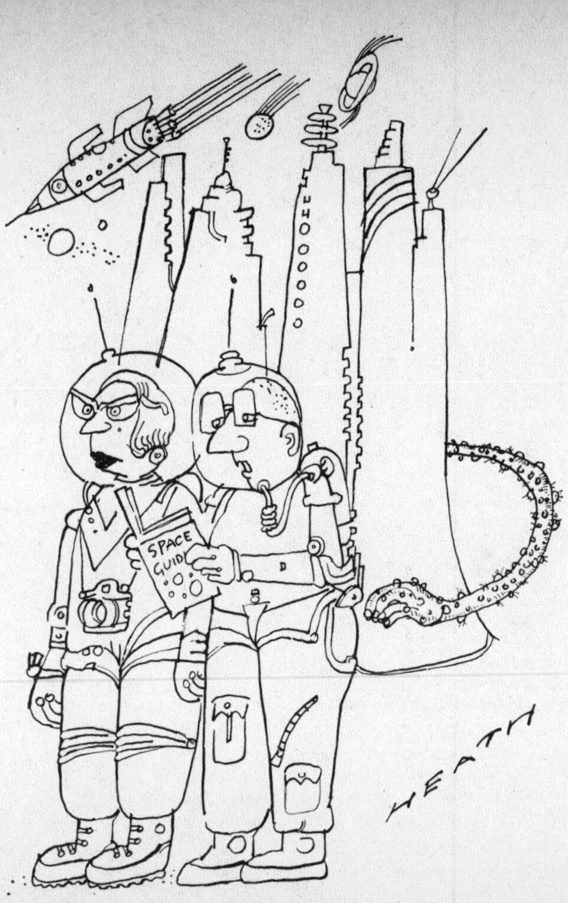

"It says here we should beware of local pickpockets."

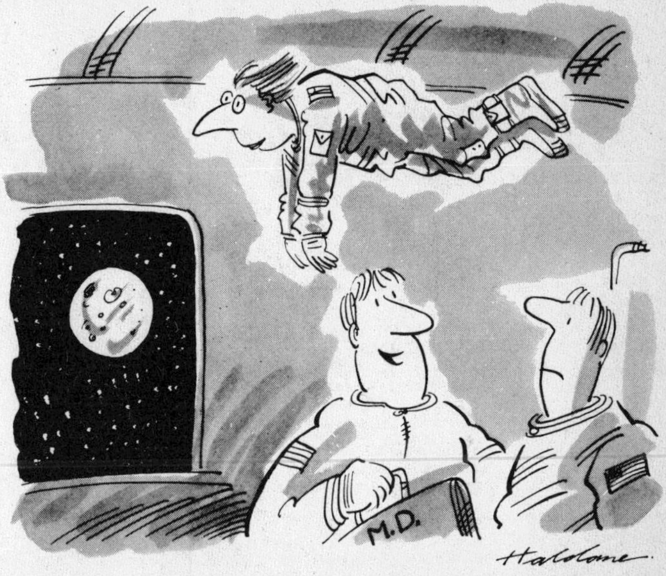

"Actually, we're not weightless. He's on Valium."

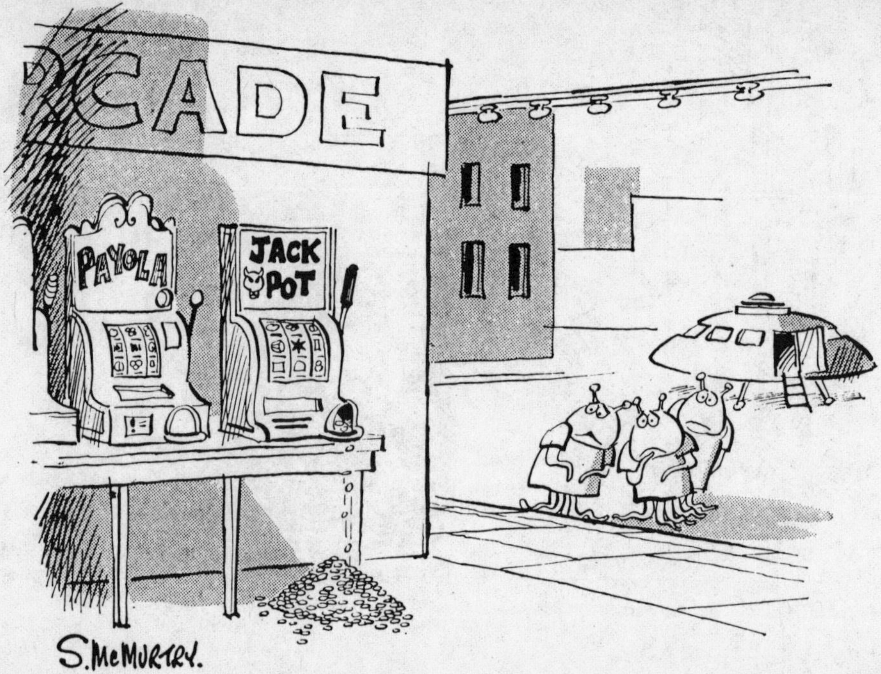

"I just shook his hand and he was sick."

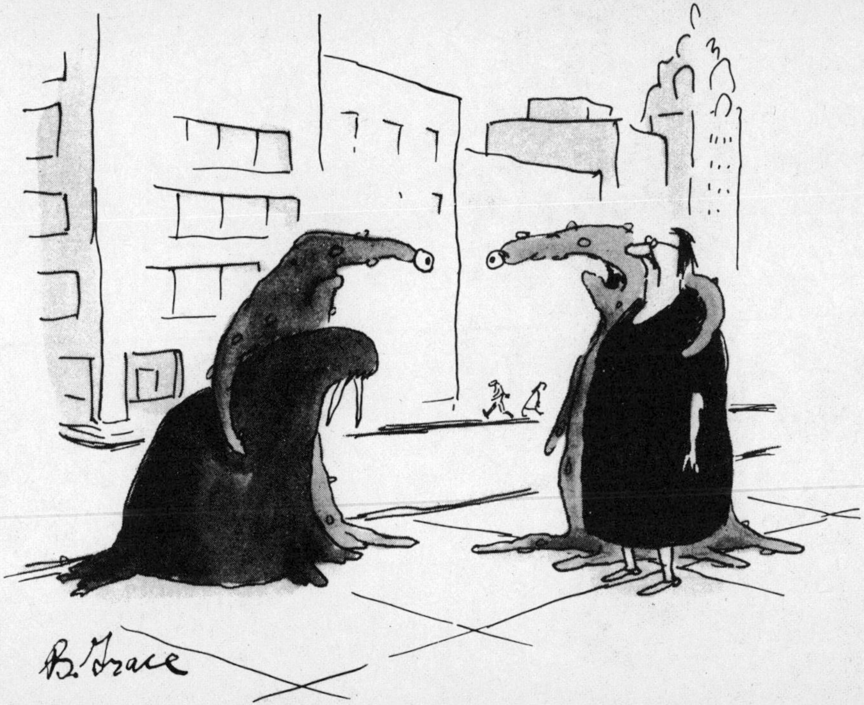

"That's the way it is down here – they're either ugly or they don't know how to cook."

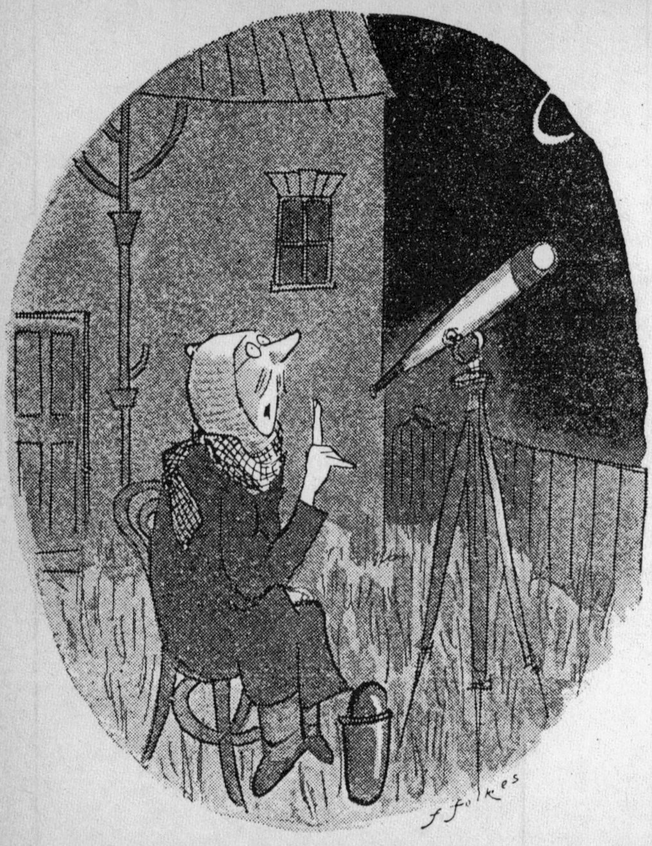

"I name you Pilkington's Comet!"

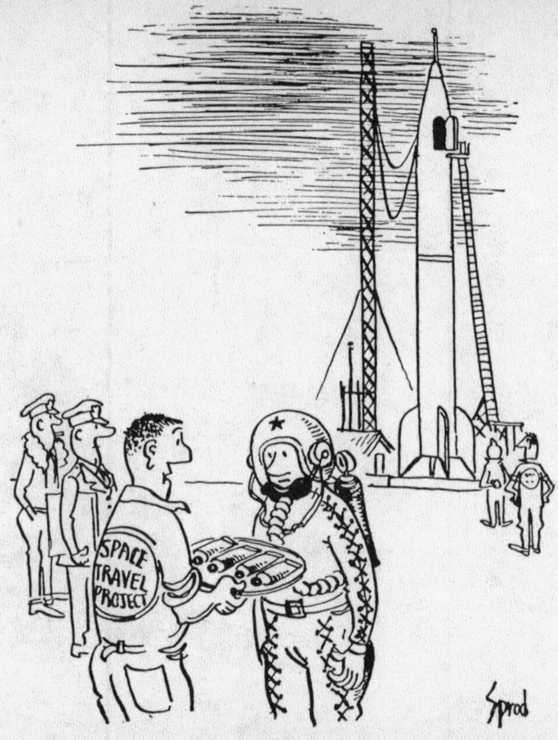

"Here are your rations for the trip – tomato soup, boiled beef and carrots, home-made apple pie, and the one on the end is toothpaste."

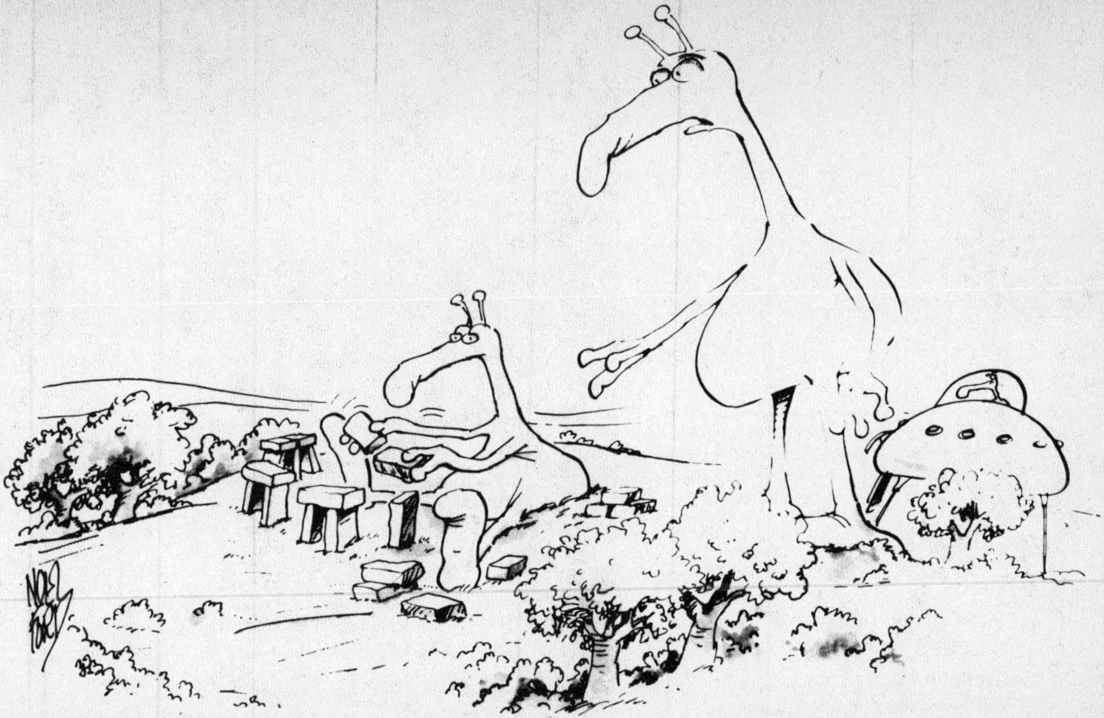

"Come along, dear, we're off now."

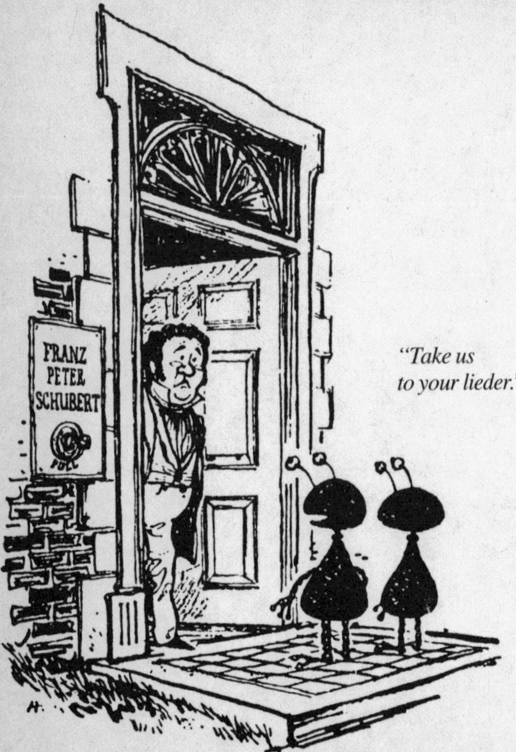

"Take us
to your lieder."

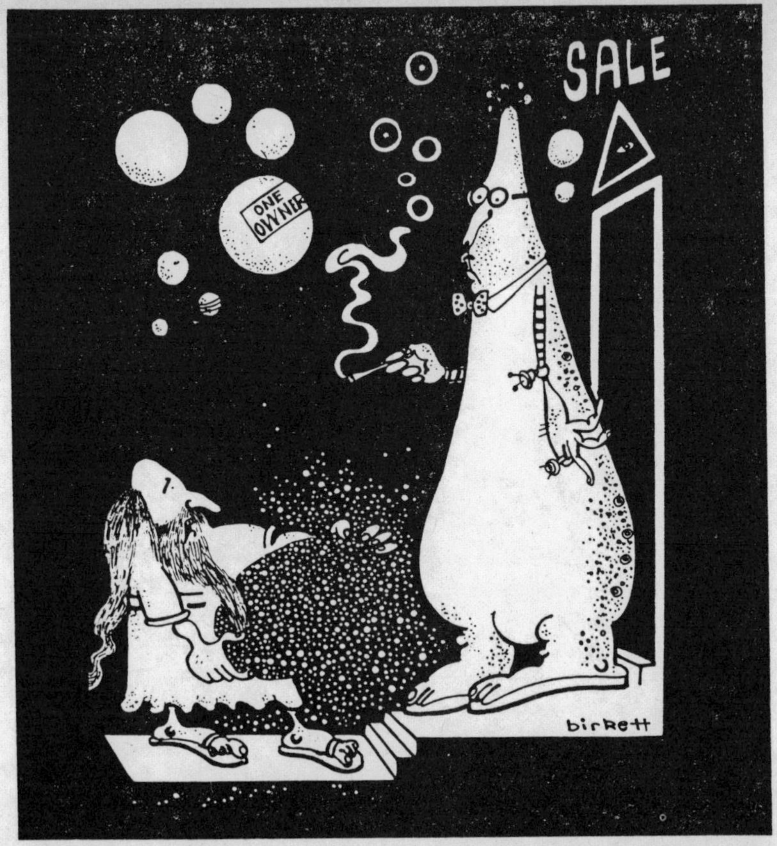

"Look here, this Universe you sold me – it's expanding!"

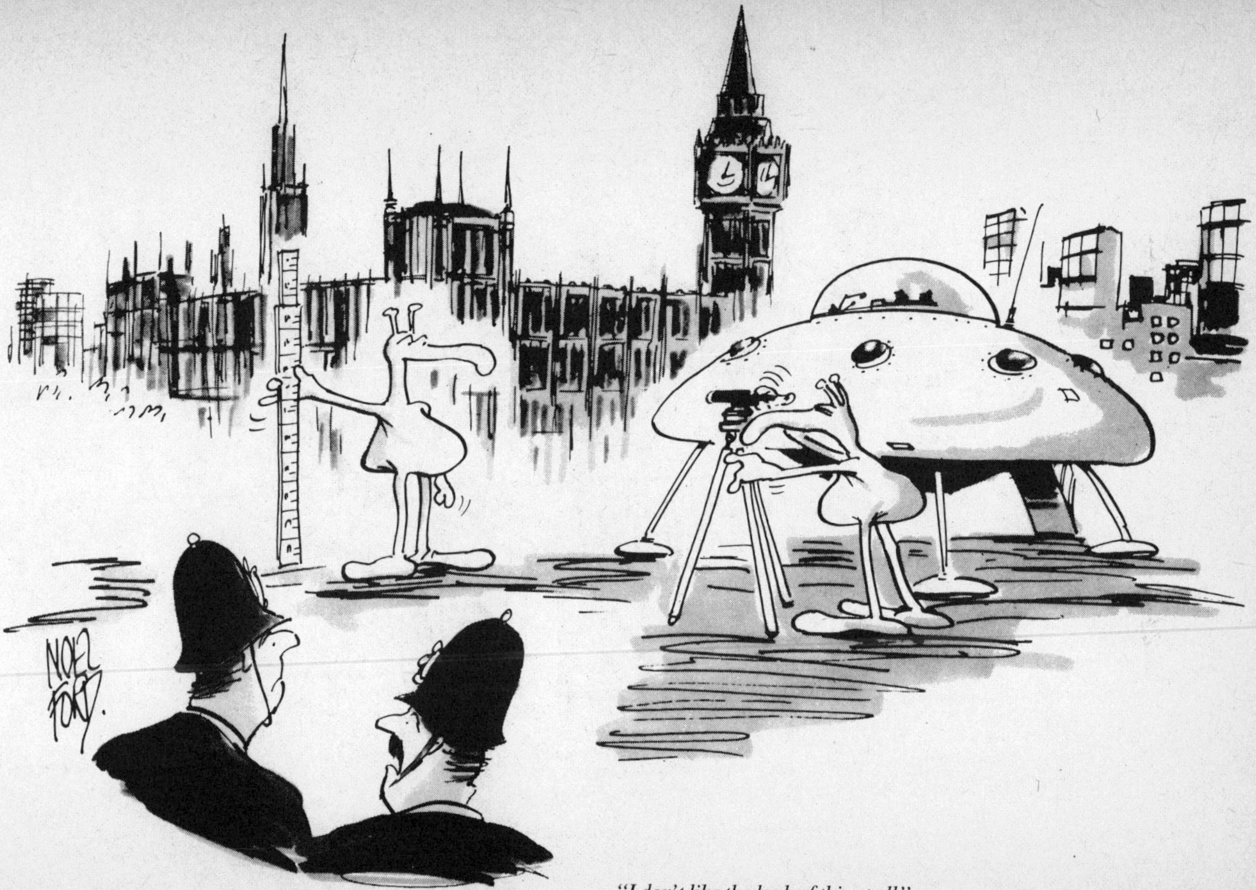

"I don't like the look of this at all."

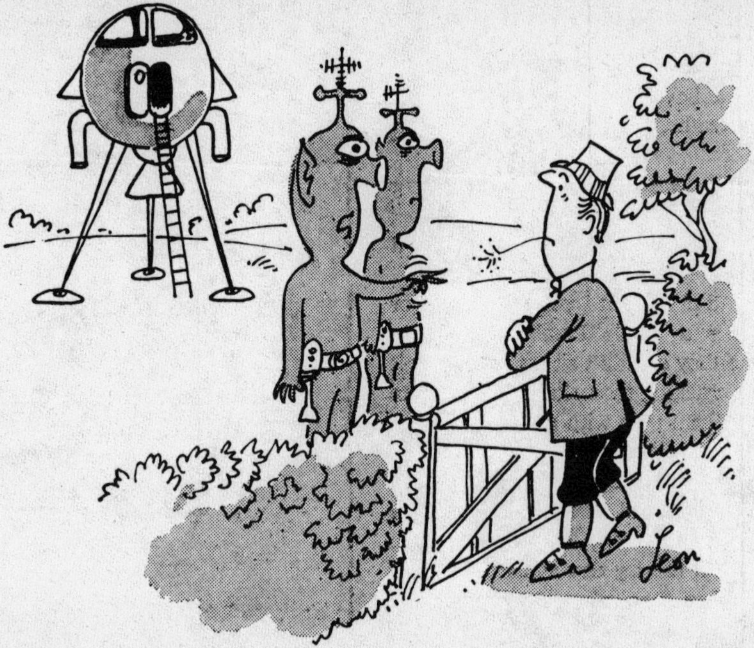

"White man speak with forked tongue!"

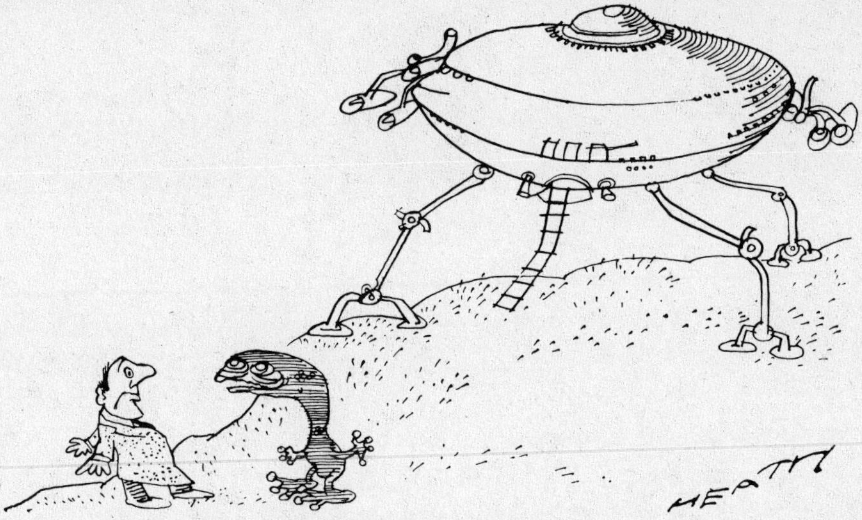

"Take me to a film producer."

CHELM OF TRYG 2, British Space Station of the Future by Bill Tidy

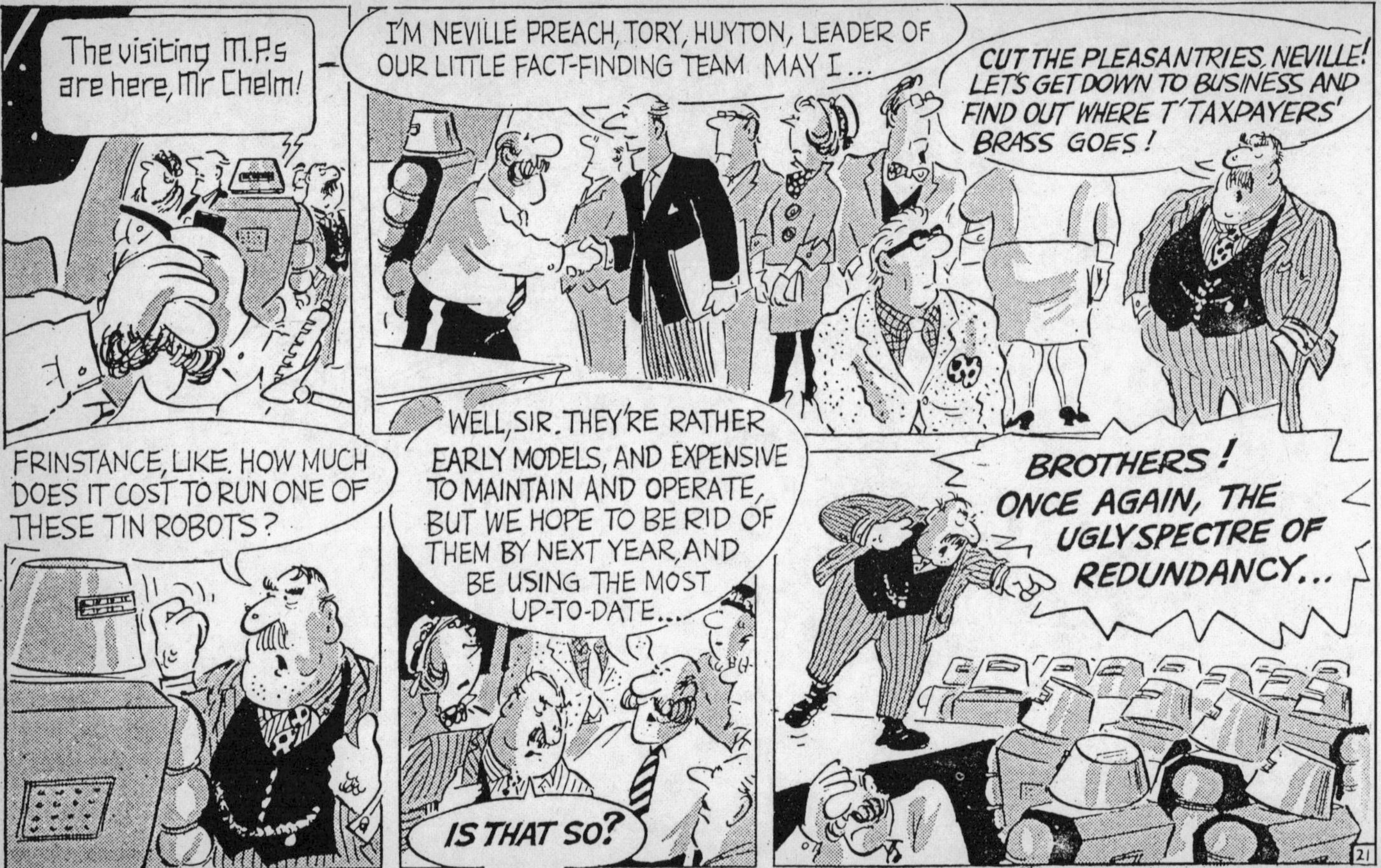

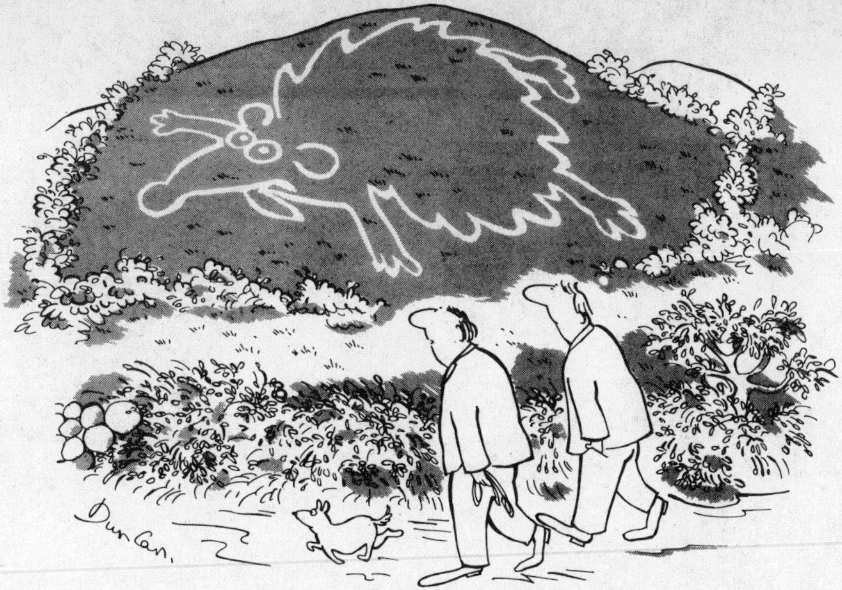

"According to the theory, a spaceship landed there 20,000 years ago."

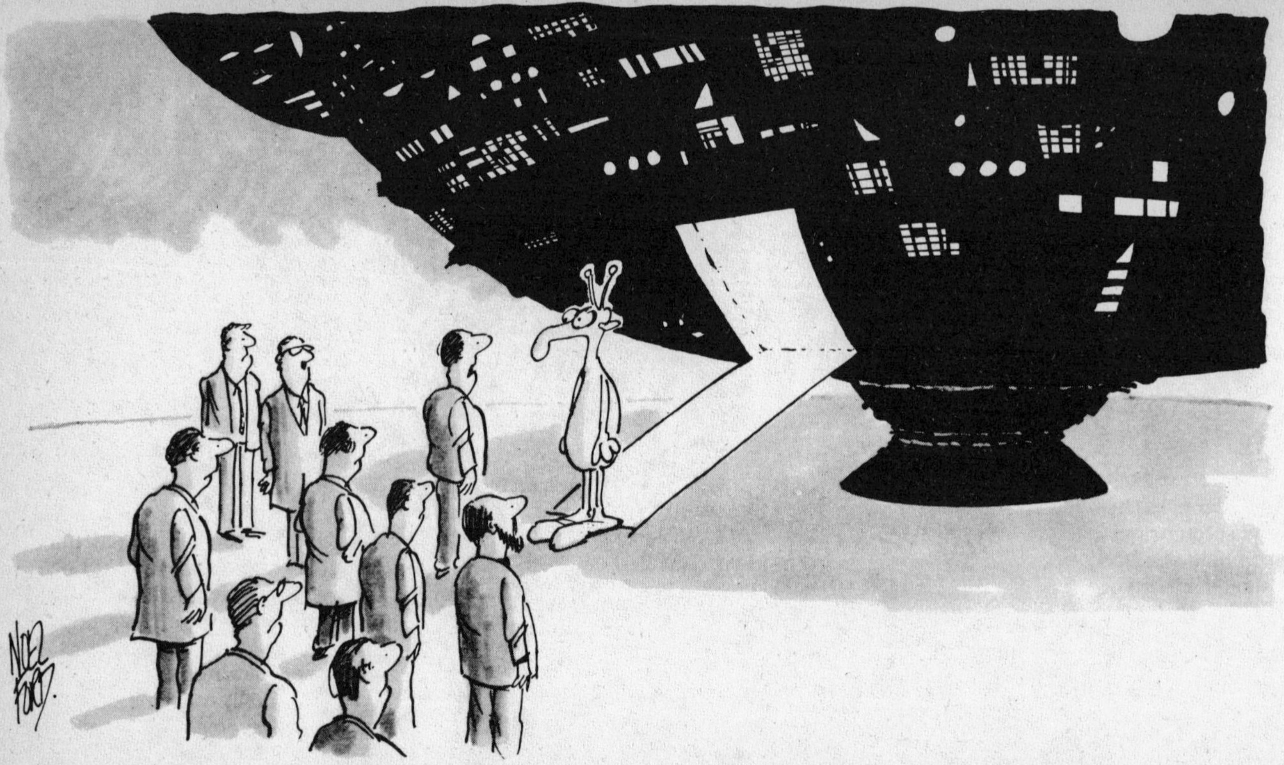

"We were rather hoping for a deep insight into trans-galactic space drive technology – we already have glass beads."

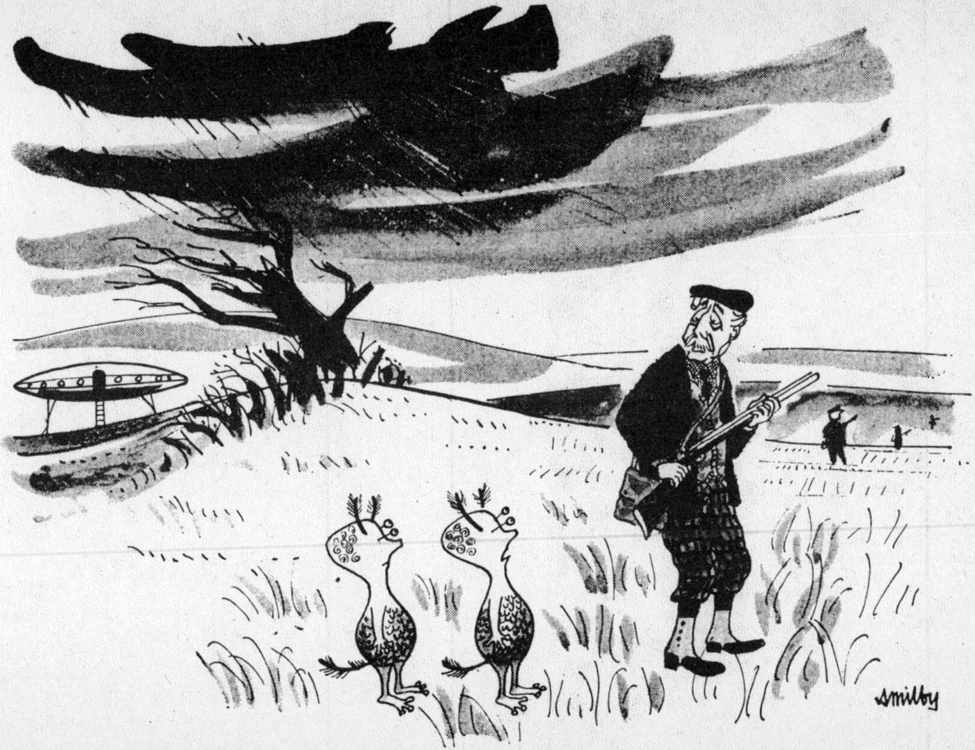

"Take us to your leader."

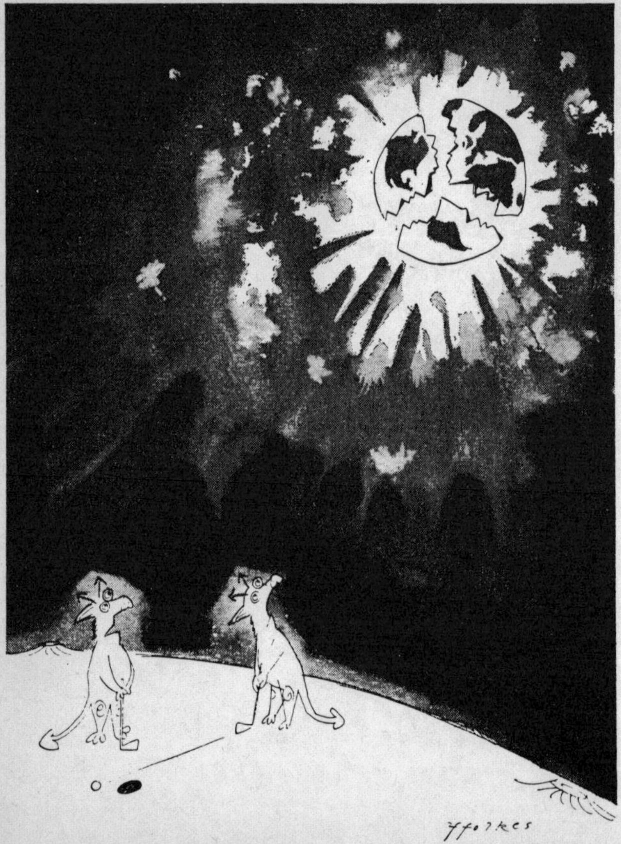

"All right. I'll allow you to play the stroke again."

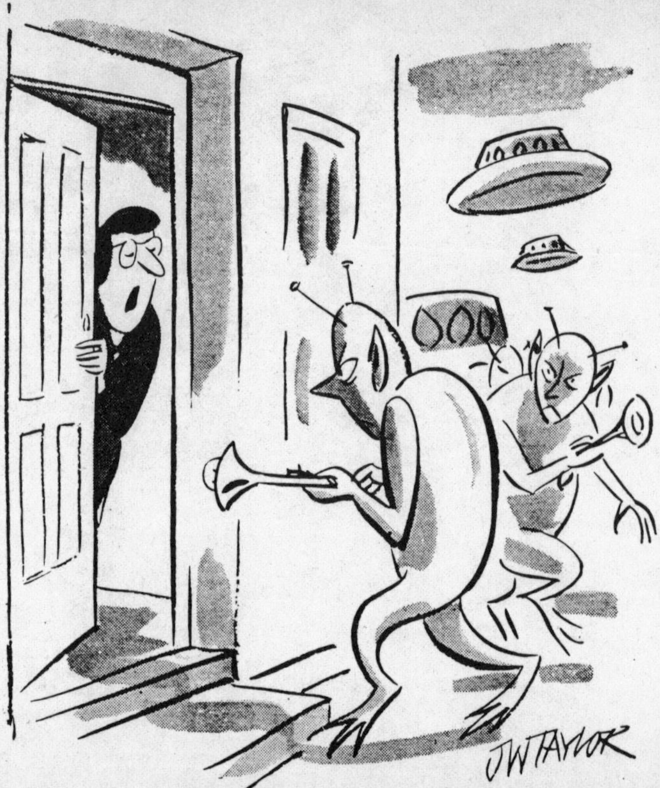

"Sorry, no coloureds."

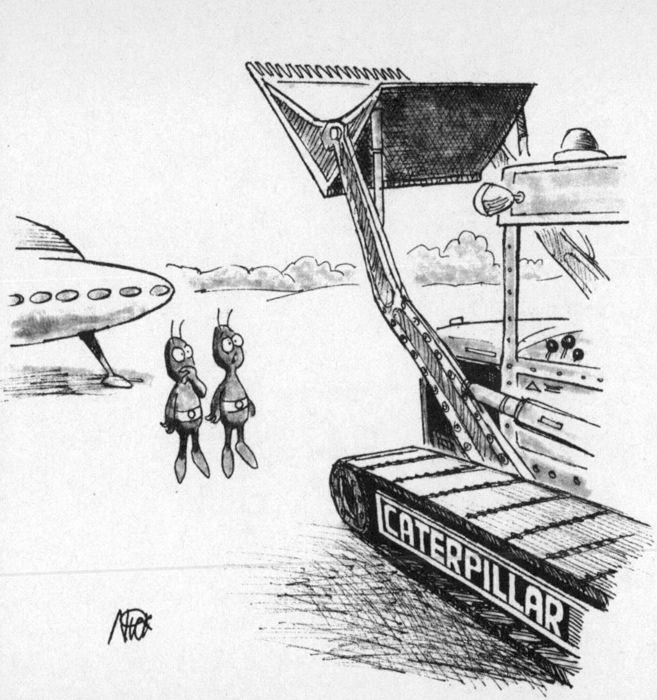

"Holy Jupiter! I hope we don't meet any of their butterflies."

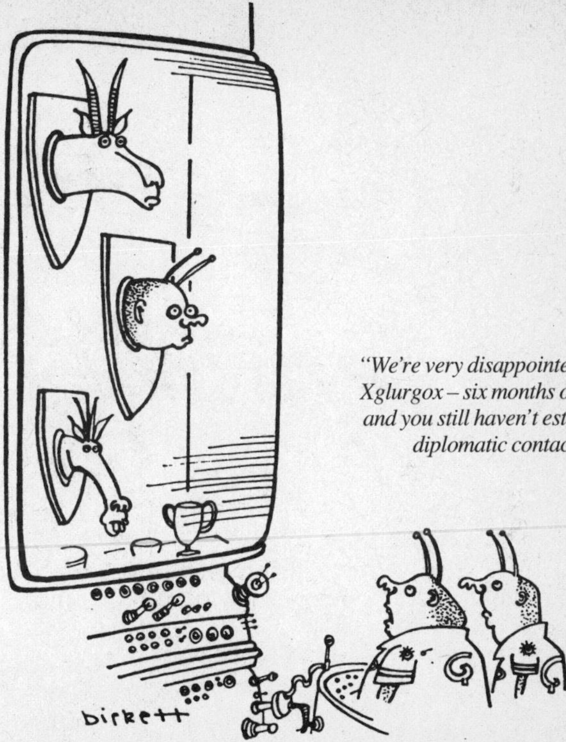

"We're very disappointed in you, Xglurgox – six months on Earth, and you still haven't established diplomatic contact."

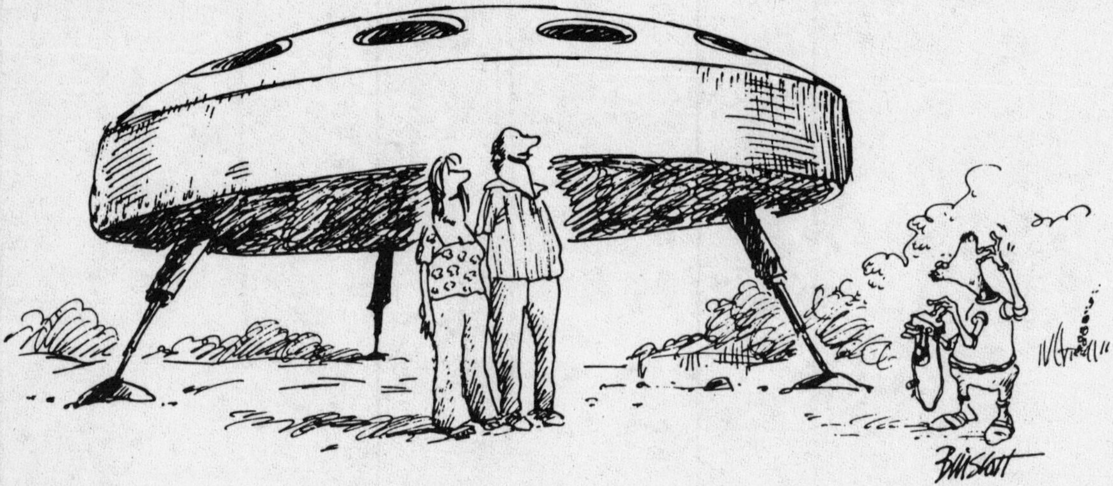

"Keep still – he's nearly got it."

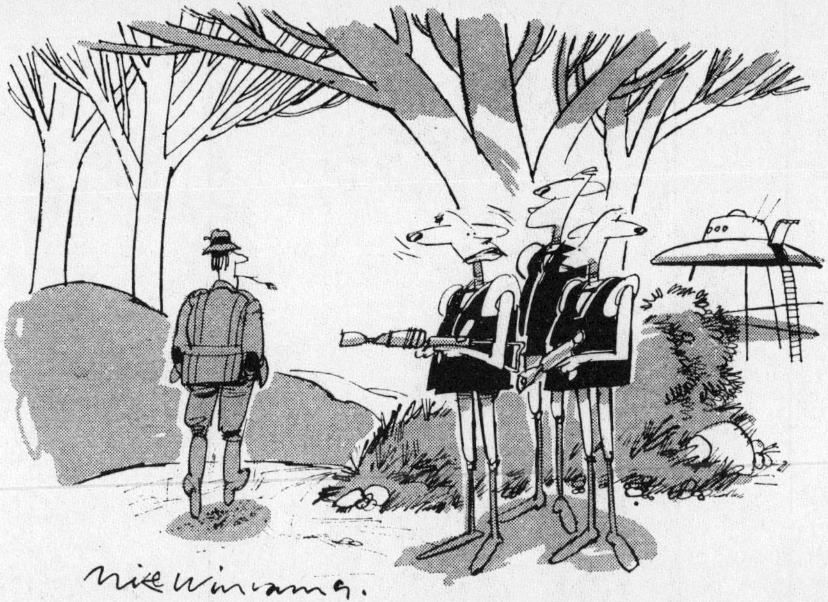

"What's he mean, 'Bloody students'?"

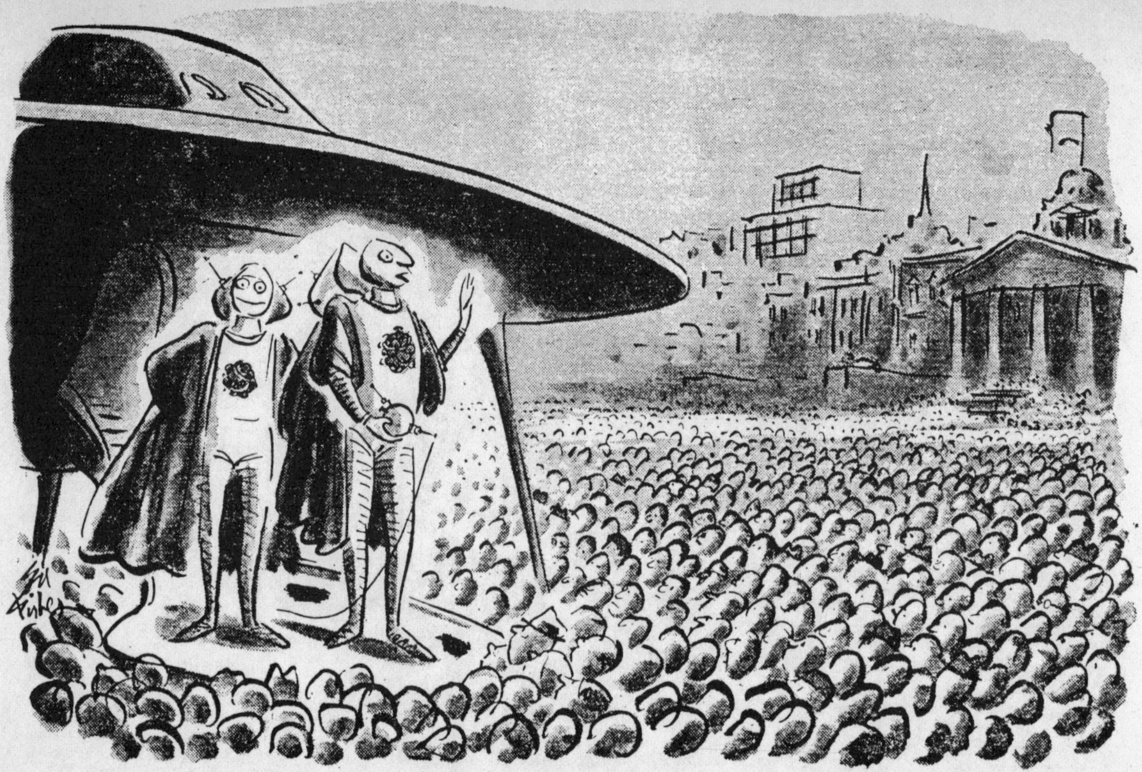

"–And our message to you humans is, grow up; settle your silly little wars; trust your fellow men; clean up the social inequities on this planet, the hunger, the disease; study; mature; apply for membership in the Galactic League of All Bipeds; make yourself worthy to join the larger planetary community and help us wipe out the damned tripedal Betelgeusians!"

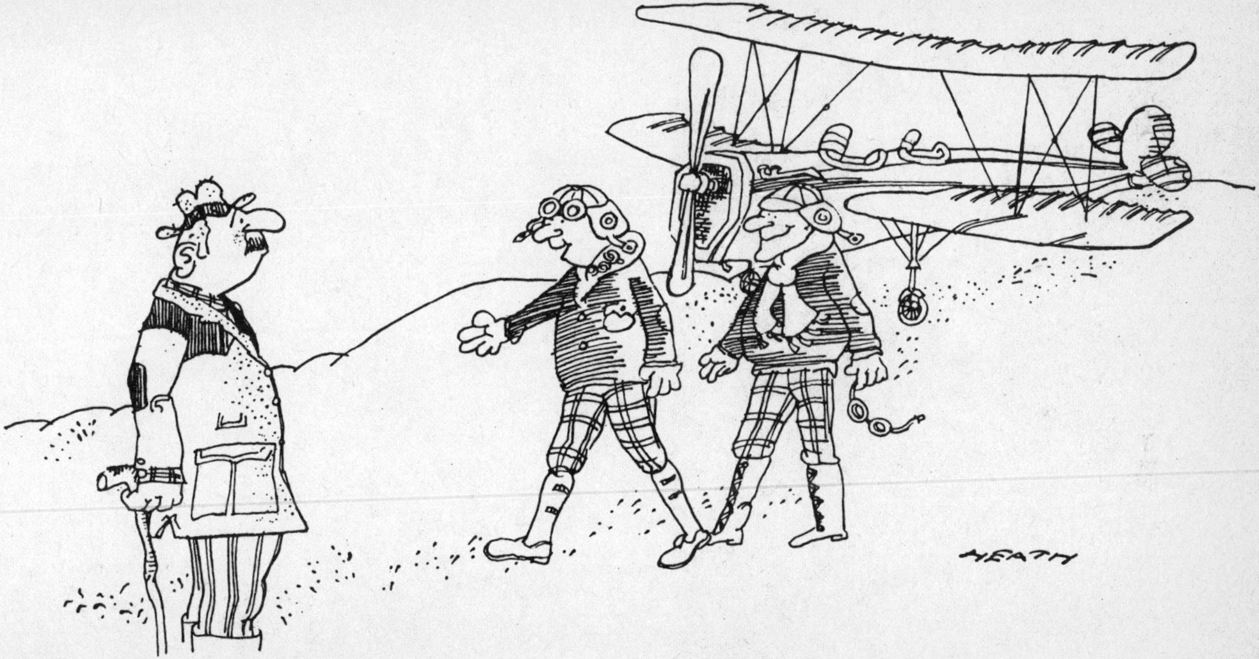

"Actually, we are from another planet, but we're not quite as advanced as you are."

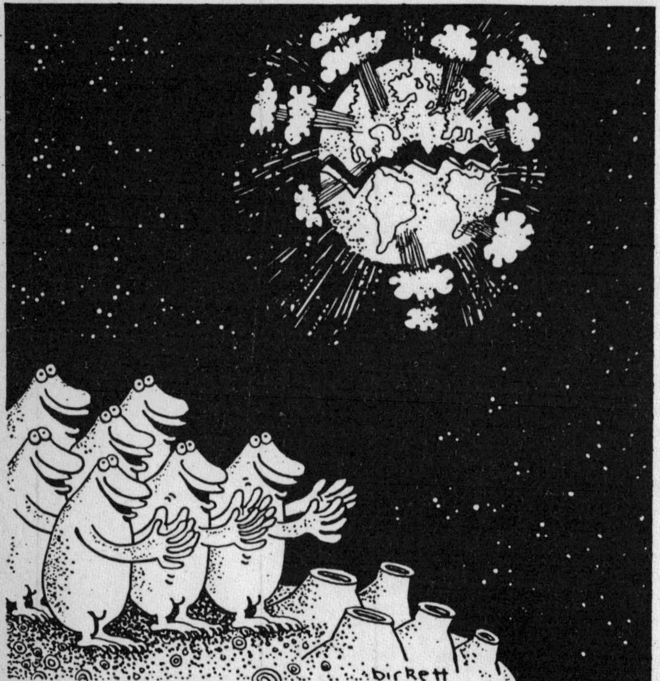

"Author! Author!"

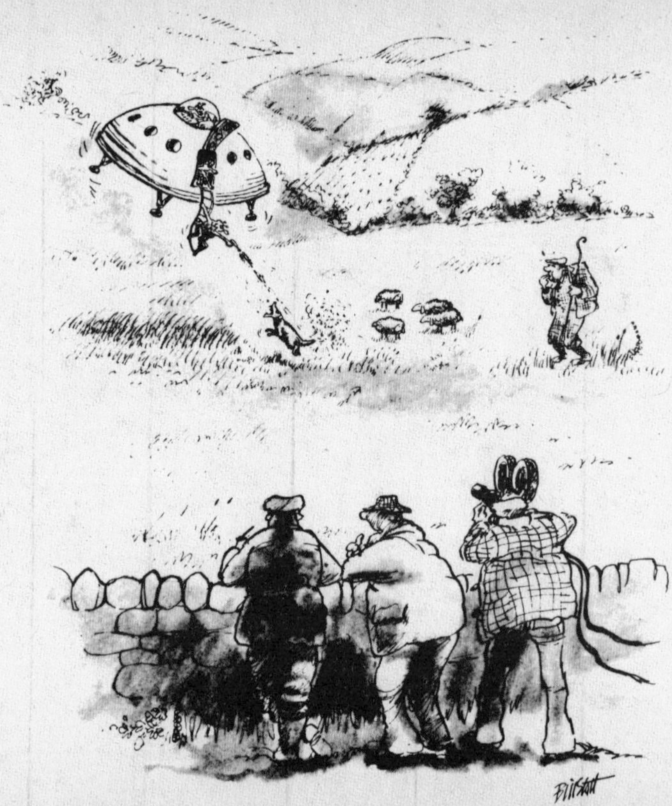

"Uh – uh! Her attention's wandered – this is costing precious points."

"Looks like they mean business this time . . ."

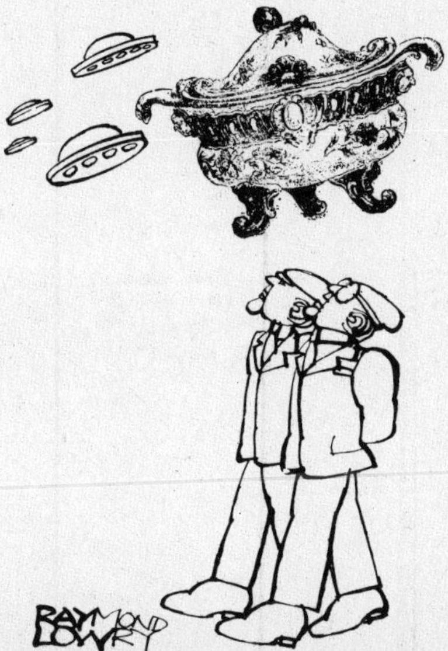

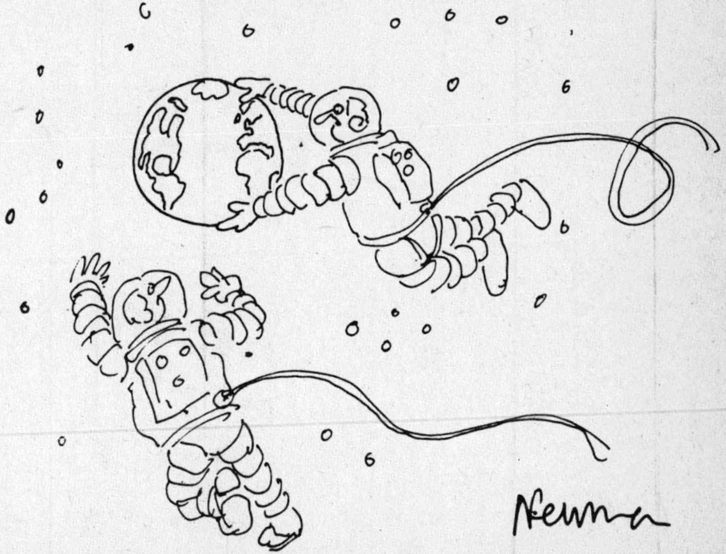

". . . but heavier than I imagined."

CHELM OF TRYG 2, British Space Station of the Future — by Bill Tidy

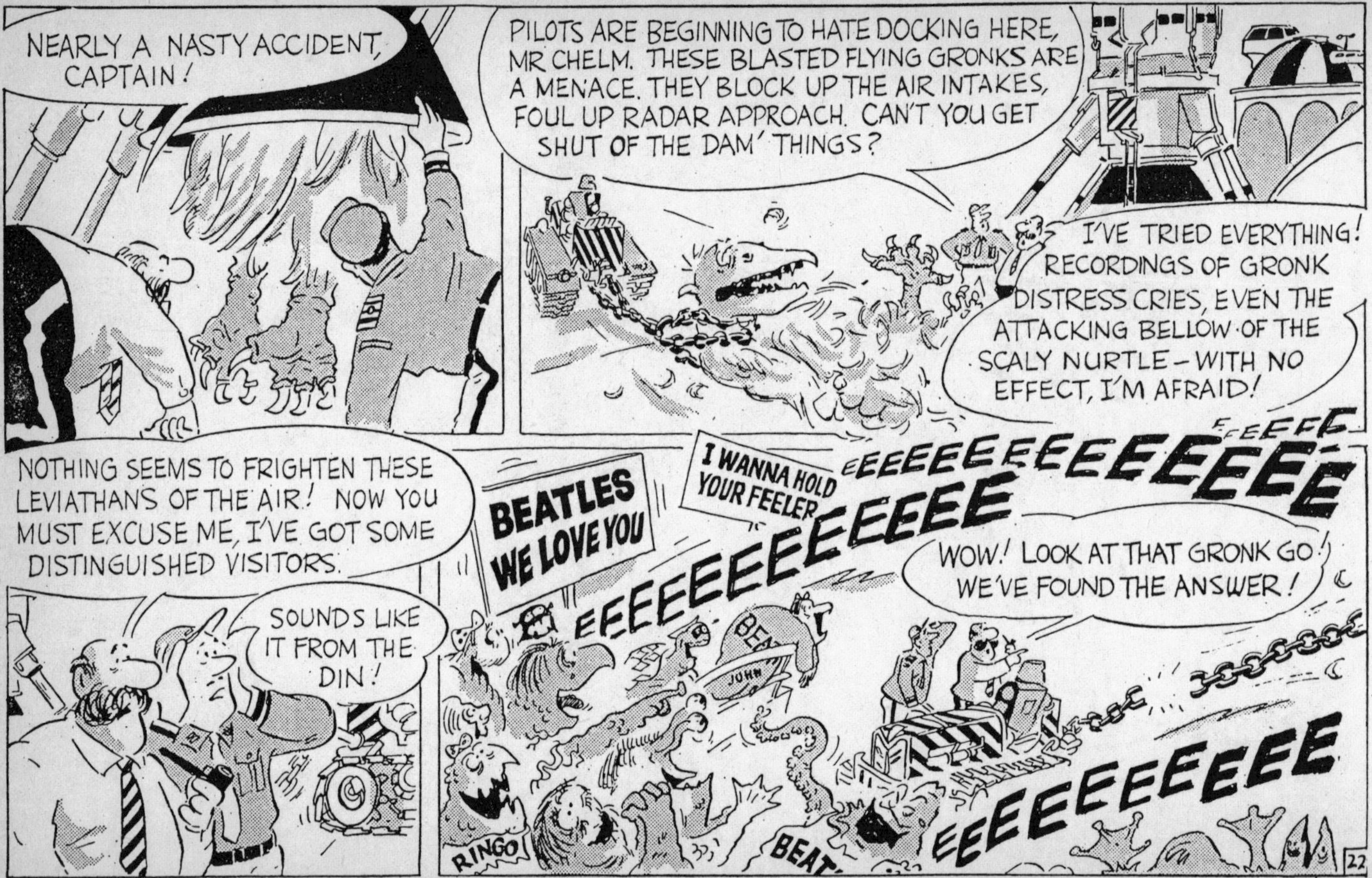

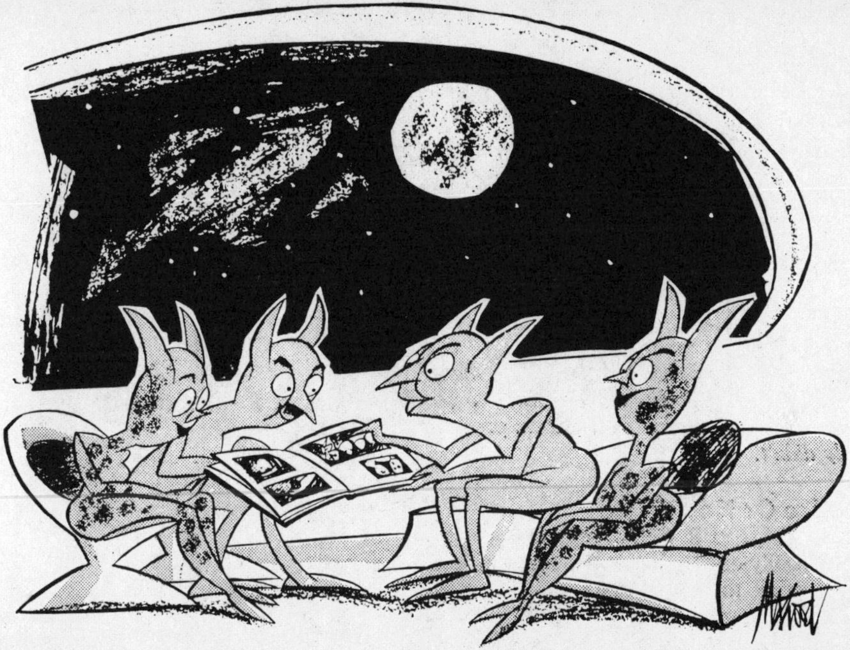

"... and this is one of the whole family taken by Frank Borman."

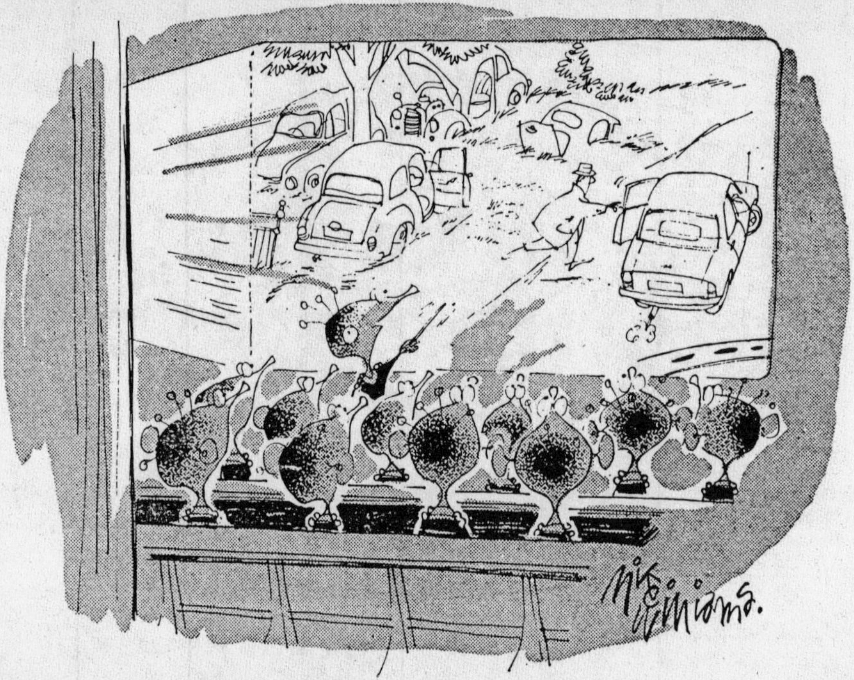

"...and every few years Earthlings go into the country and cast off their old skin."

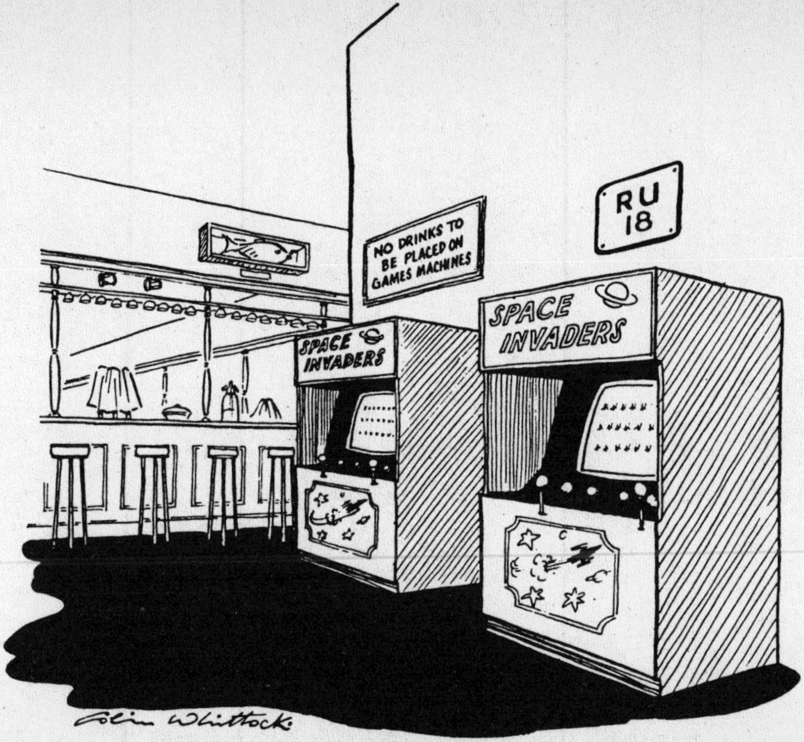

"Just think, ZXYXIL, in a very short time we will have conquered Earth!"

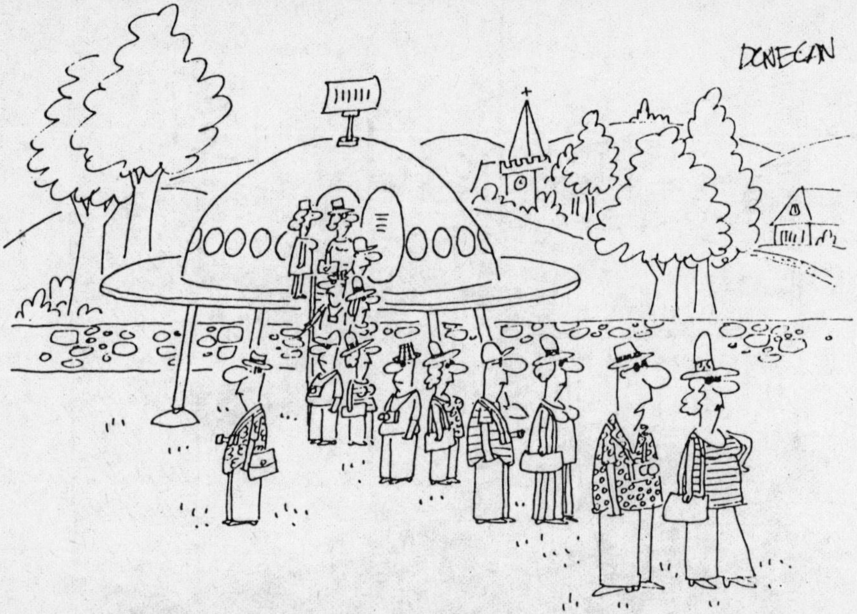

"What did I tell you? See one planet and you've seen them all."

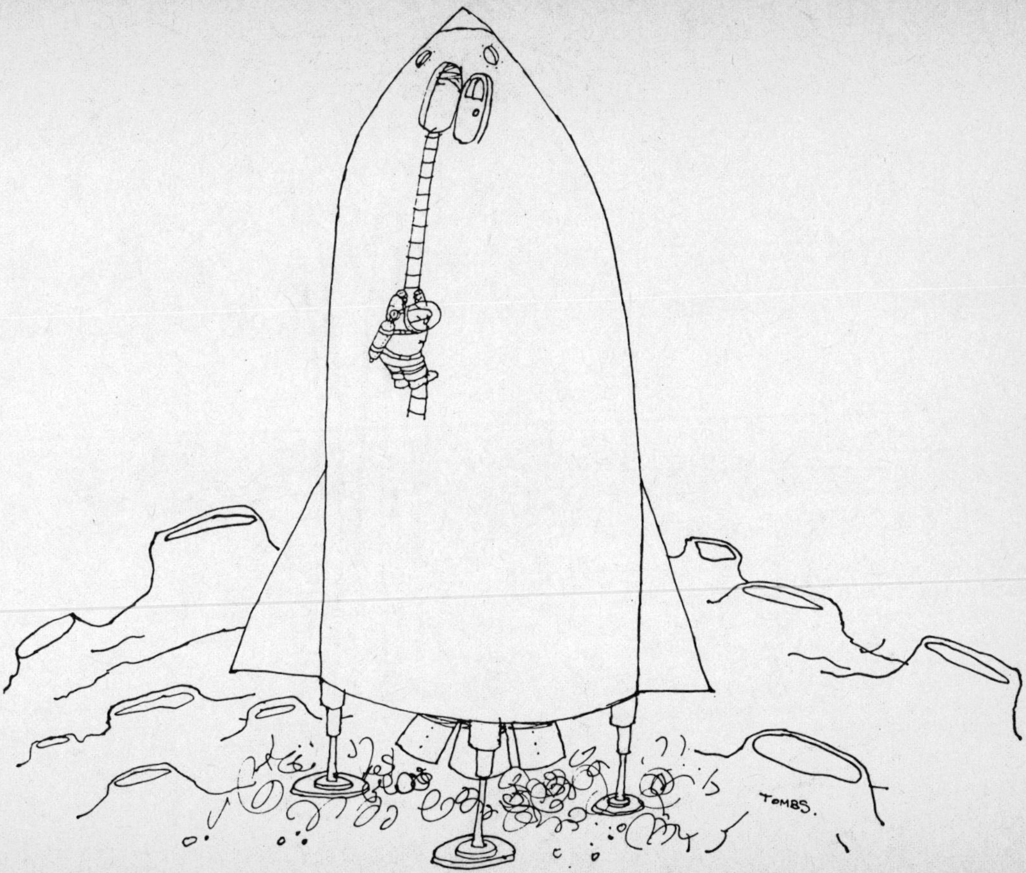
TOMBS.

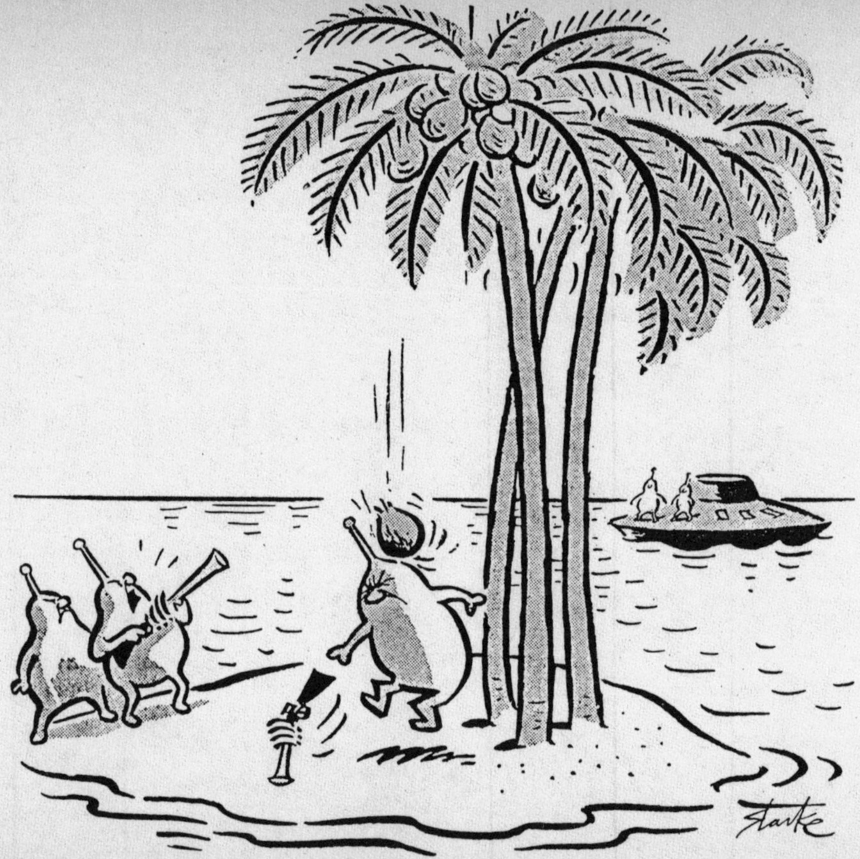

"All right – if this is the way you want it. But don't forget we came here with peaceful intentions."

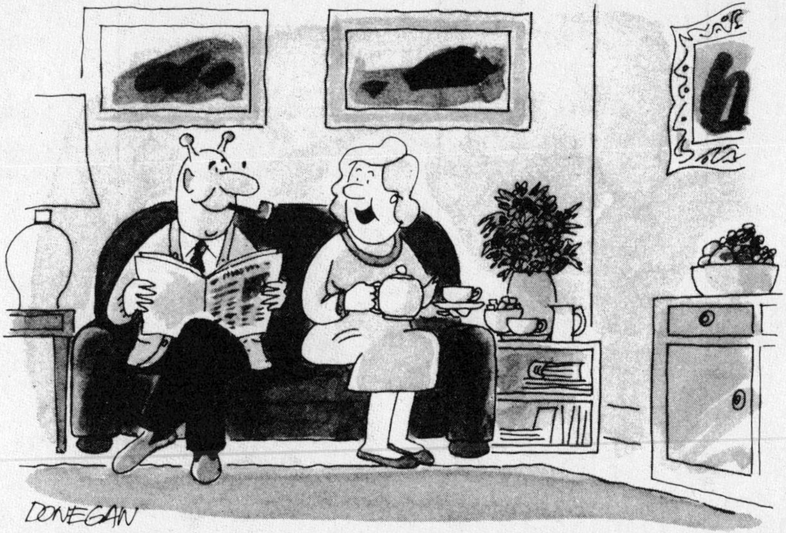

"It seems only yesterday that you walked through that wall and said, 'Greetings, Earthling!"

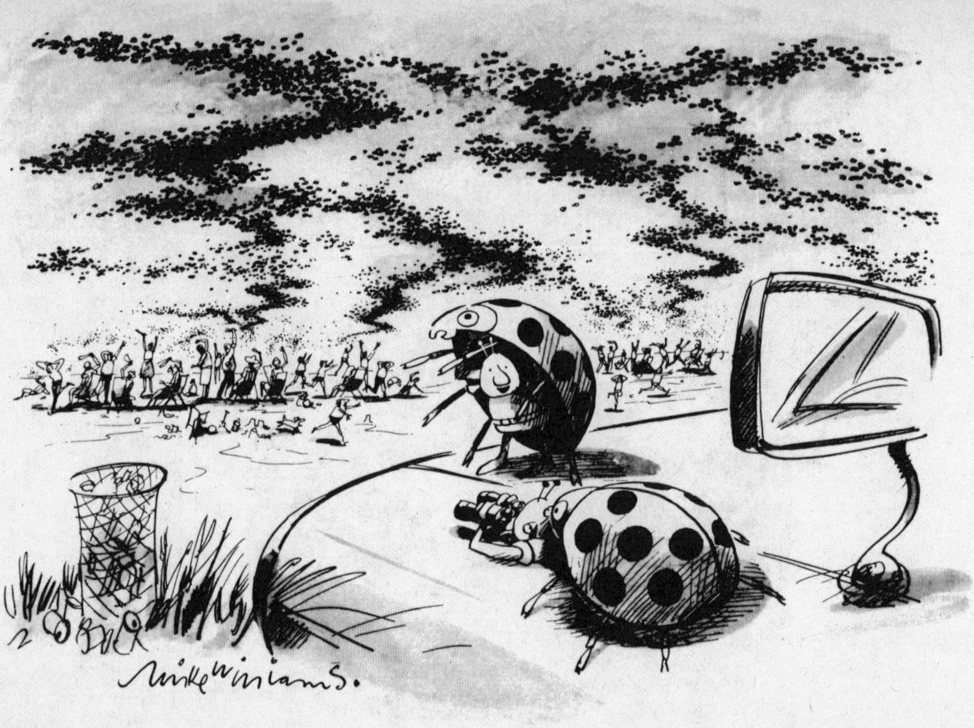

"How we doing, Otog?"

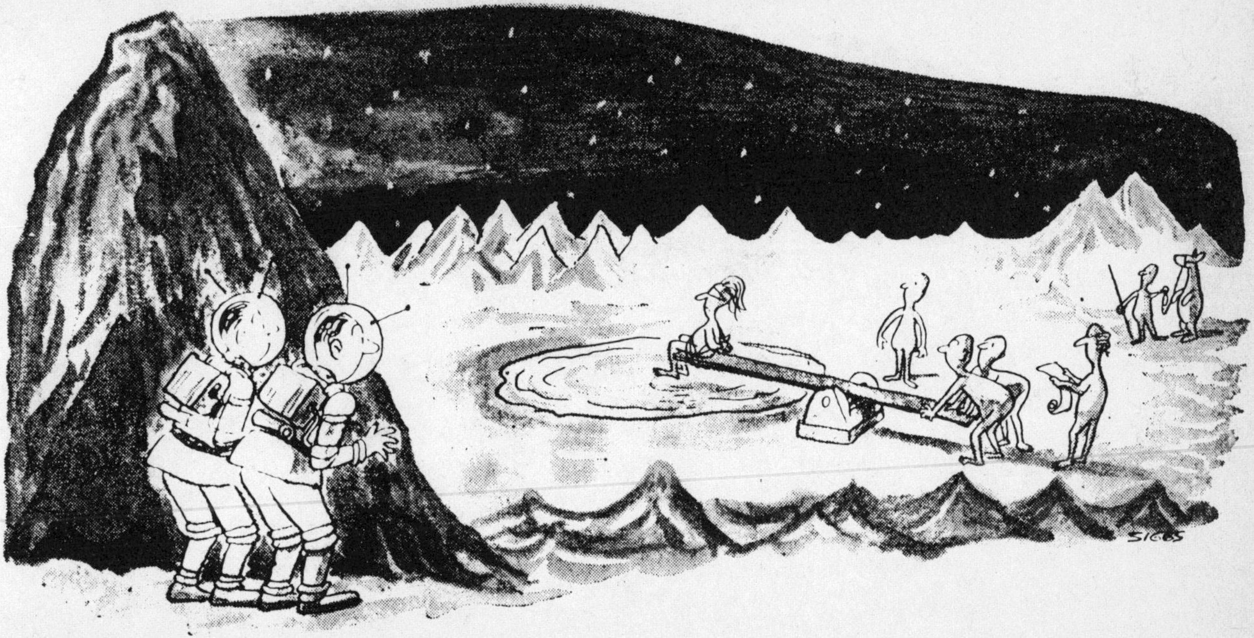
SIGGS

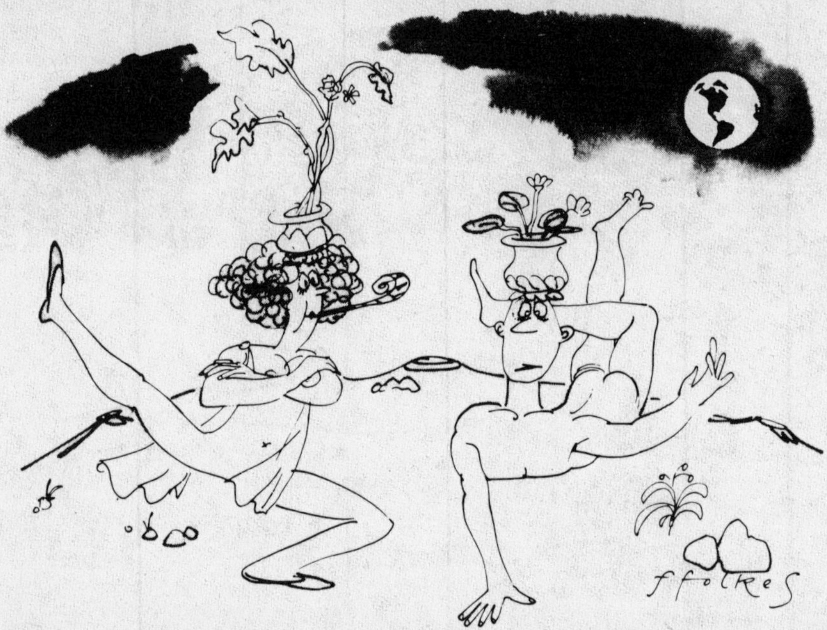

"Do you think there's intelligent life anywhere else in the Universe?"

CHELM OF TRYG 2, British Space Station of the Future

by Bill Tidy

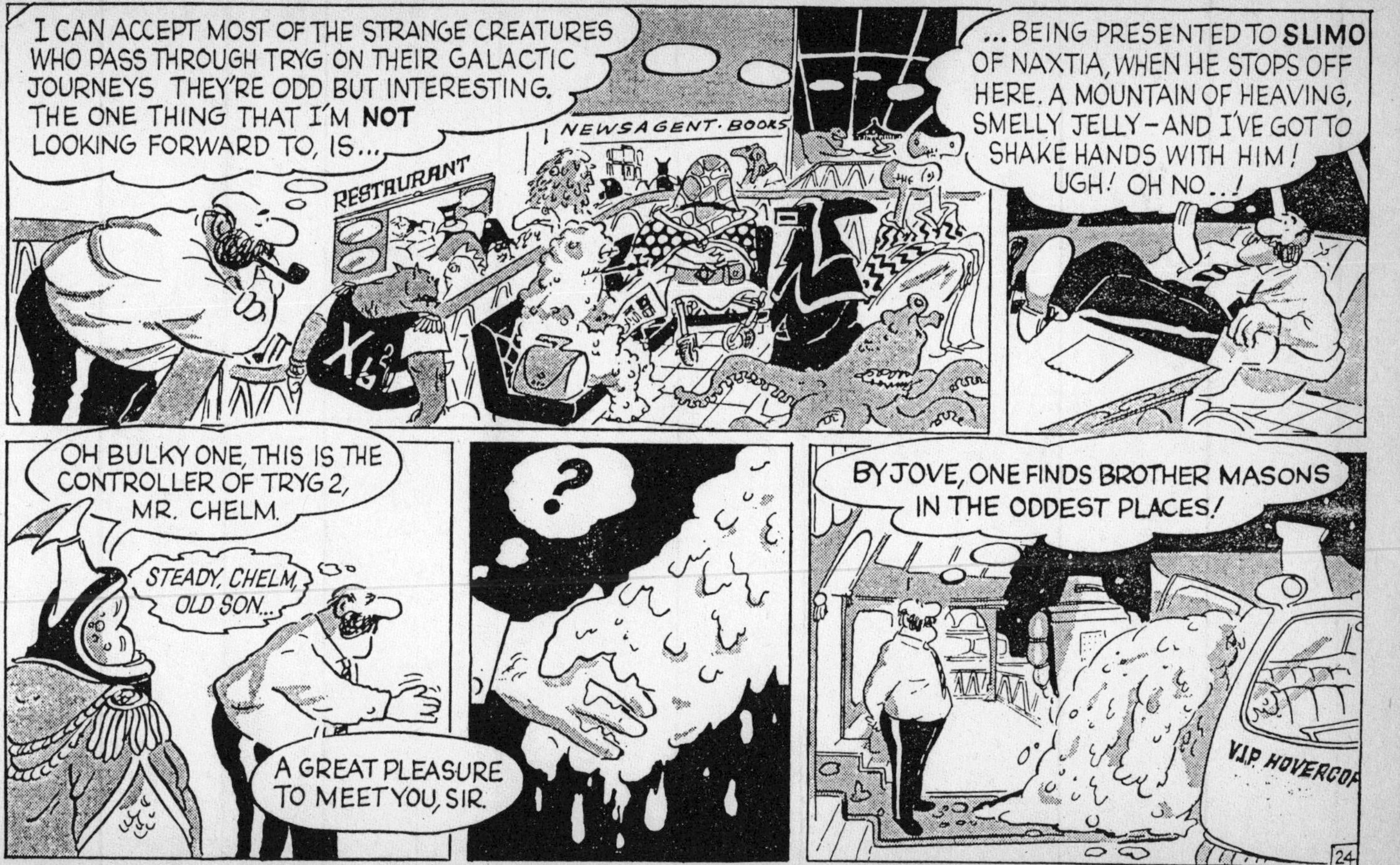

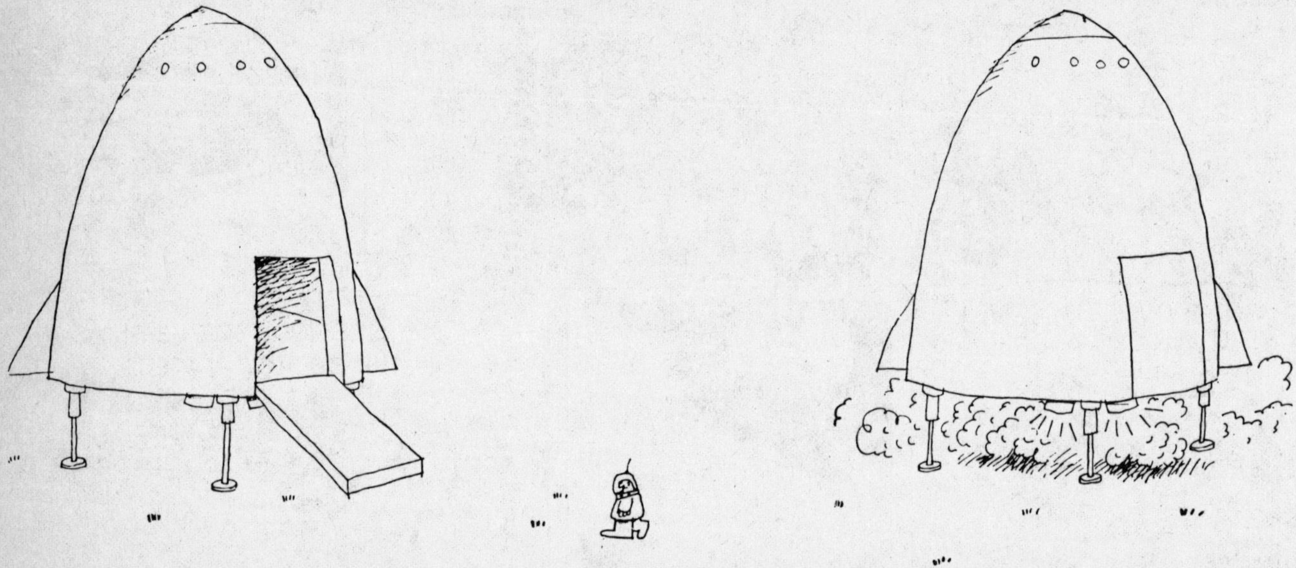

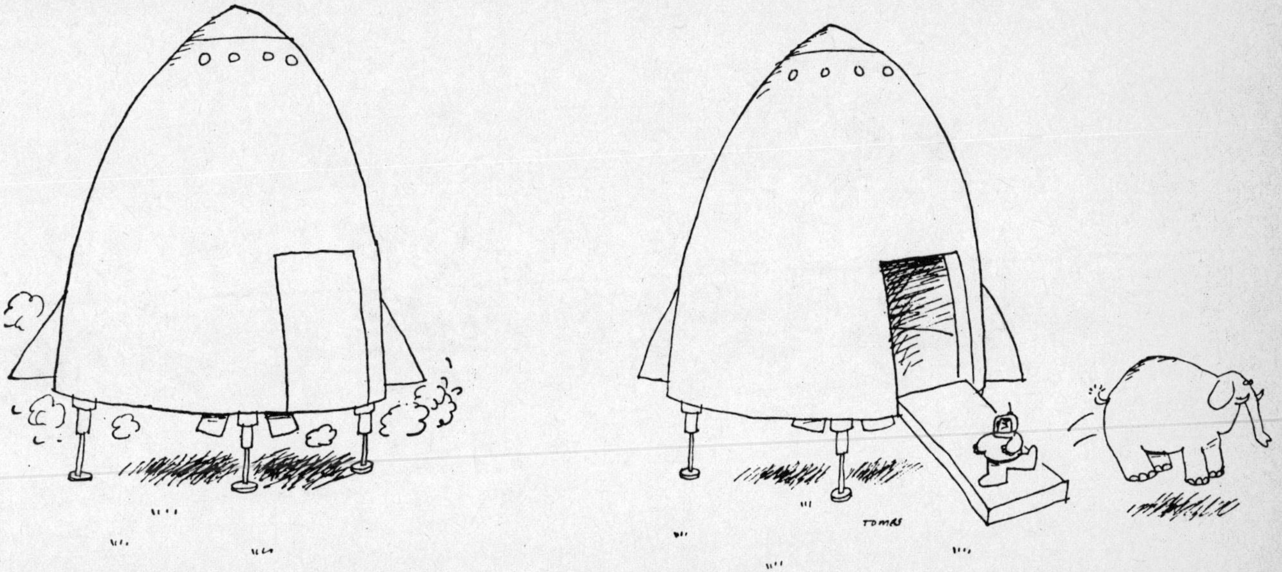

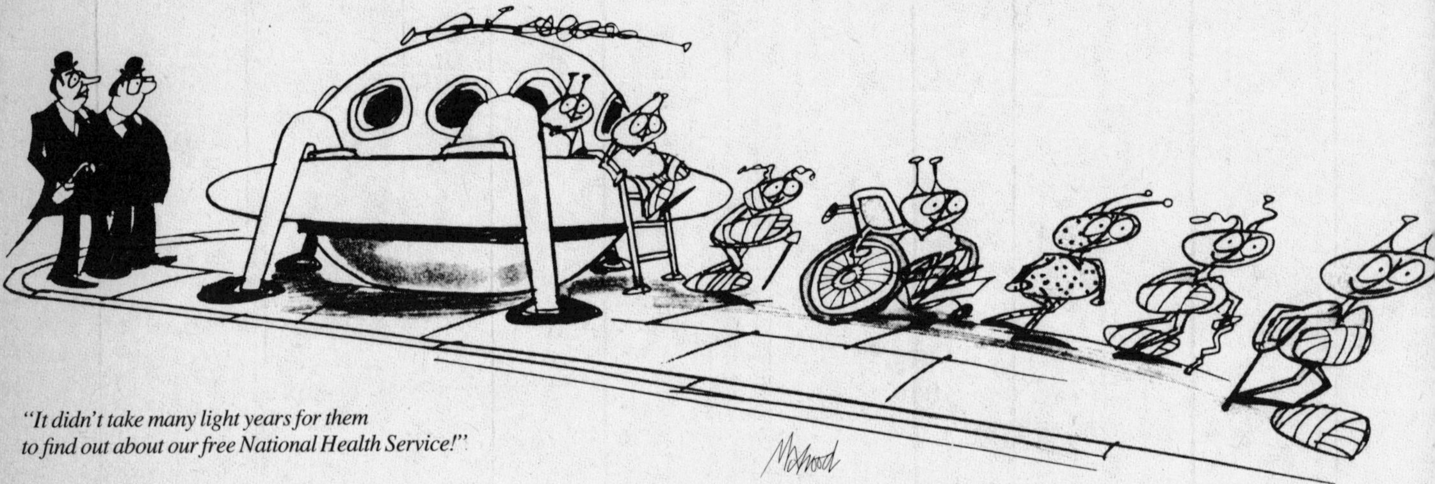

"It didn't take many light years for them to find out about our free National Health Service!"

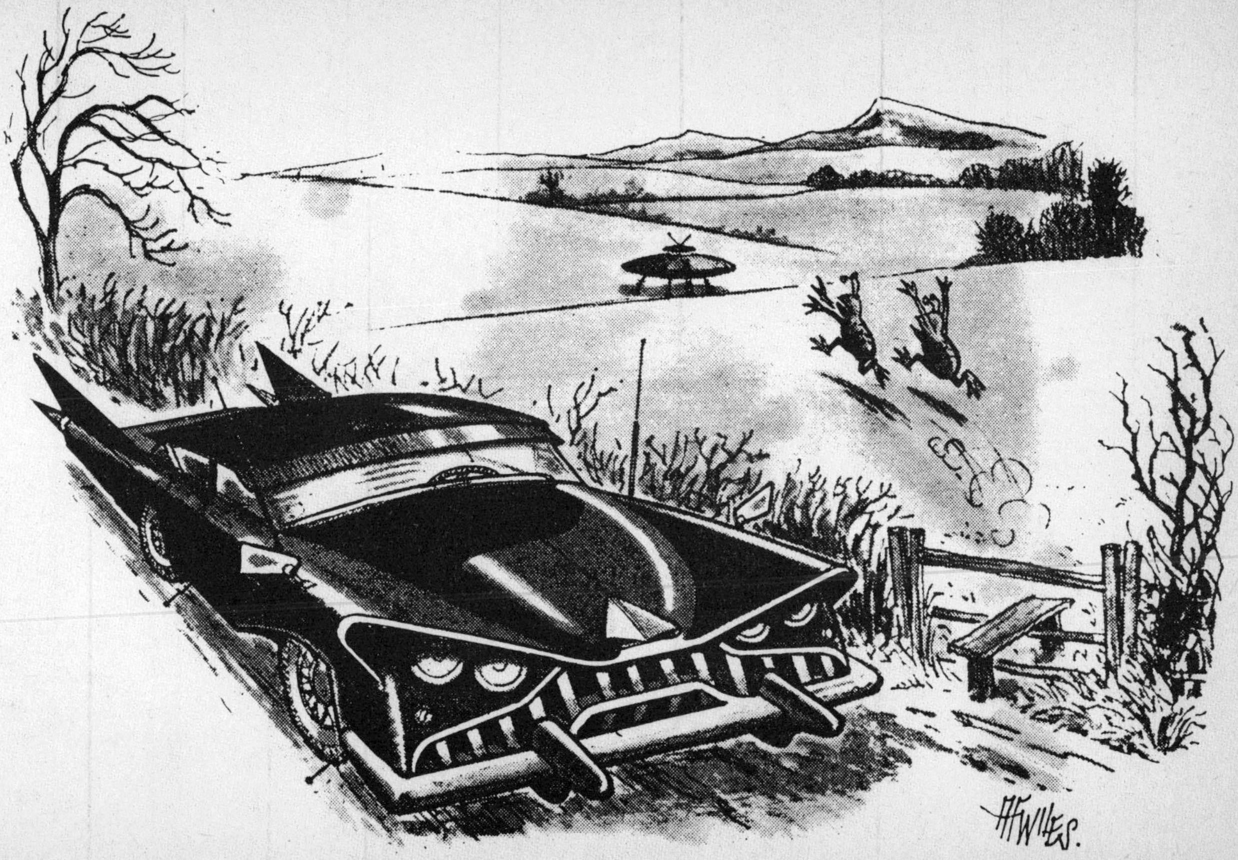

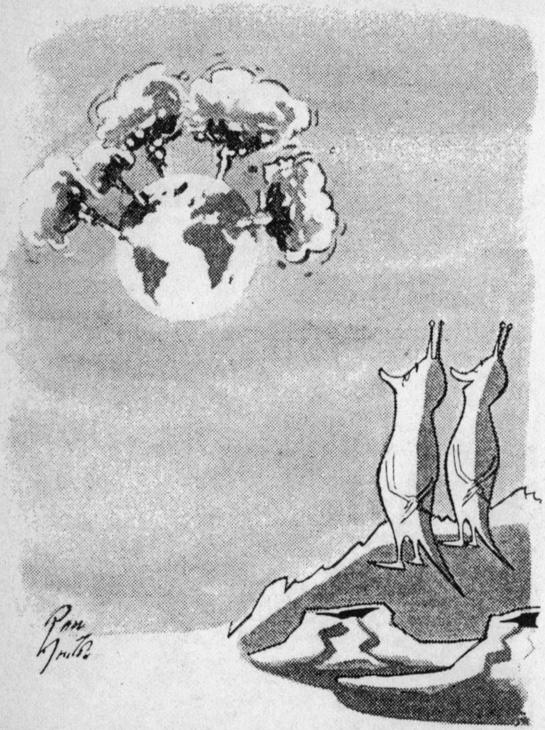

"It looks as though you've lost your bet."

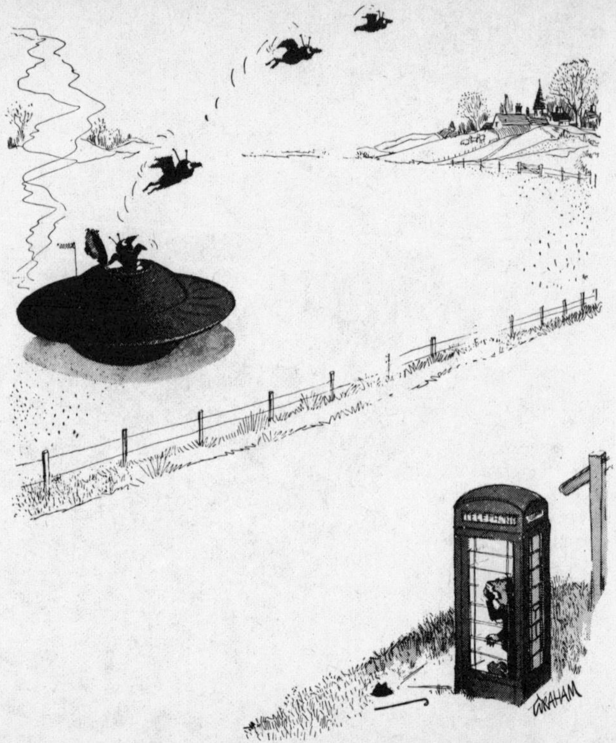

"Wait! That isn't the whole story!"

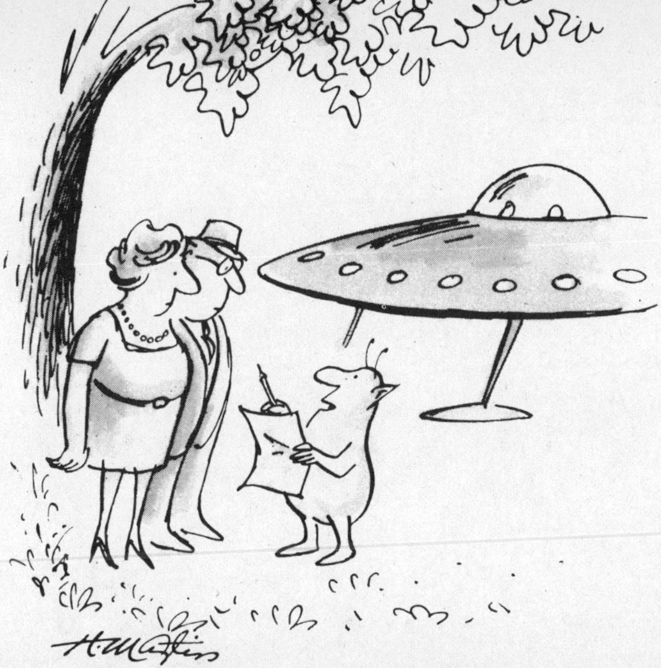

"I'll need your signatures on this. It's just a routine form – releasing us from any legal responsibility for your safety while aboard our craft."

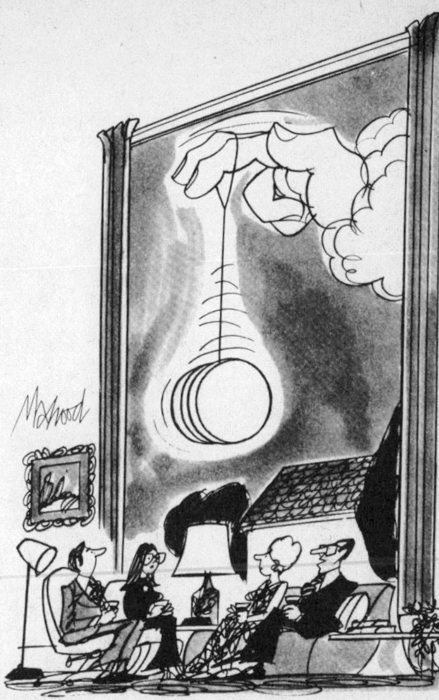

"There's no doubt creatures of a higher intelligence are trying to communicate with us – the question is, what are they trying to say?"

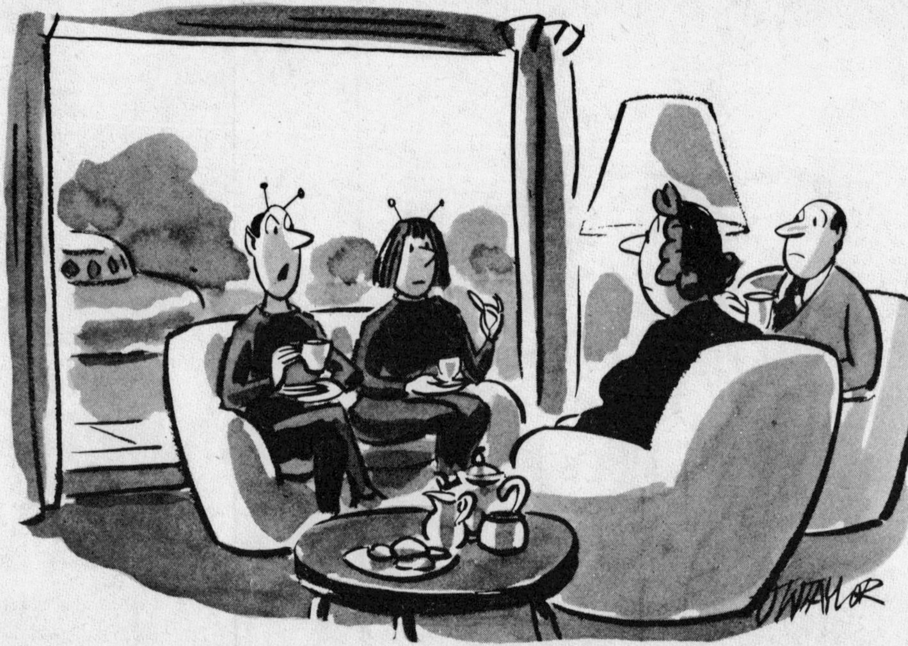

"If it comes to that,
after our movies
you're something
of an anti-climax."

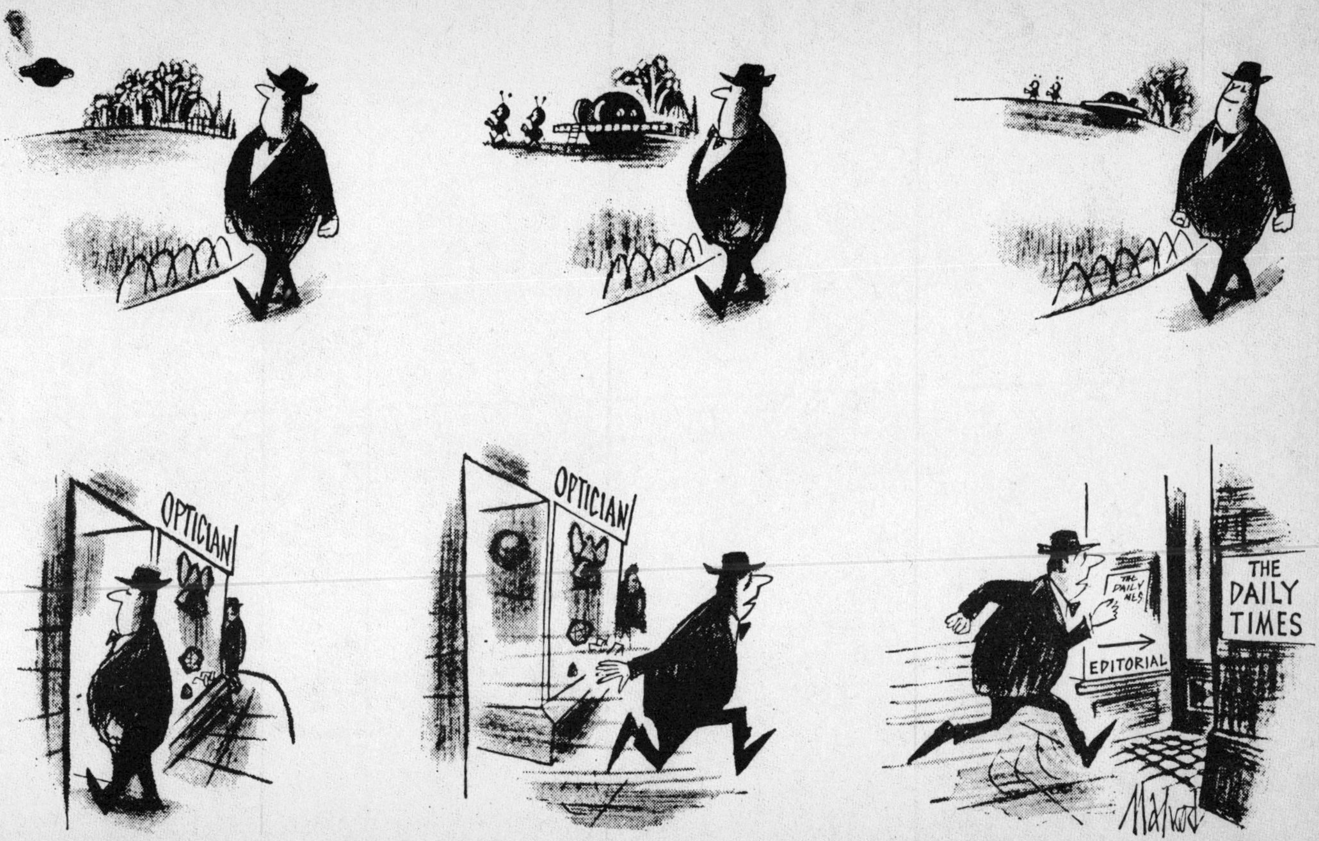
OPTICIAN
OPTICIAN
EDITORIAL
THE DAILY TIMES

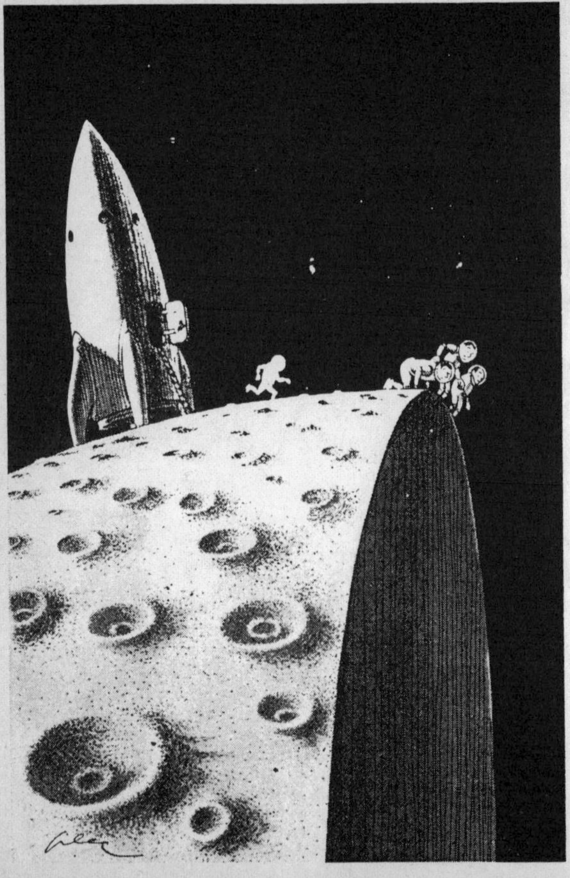

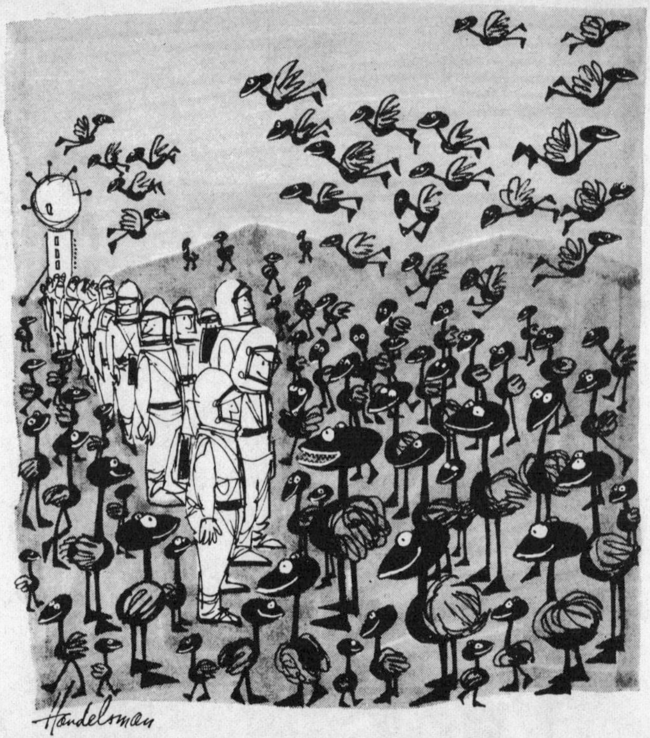

"I'm afraid you'll find us rather backward. We have wars, poverty, disease, religious and racial intolerance, and a contempt for democracy."

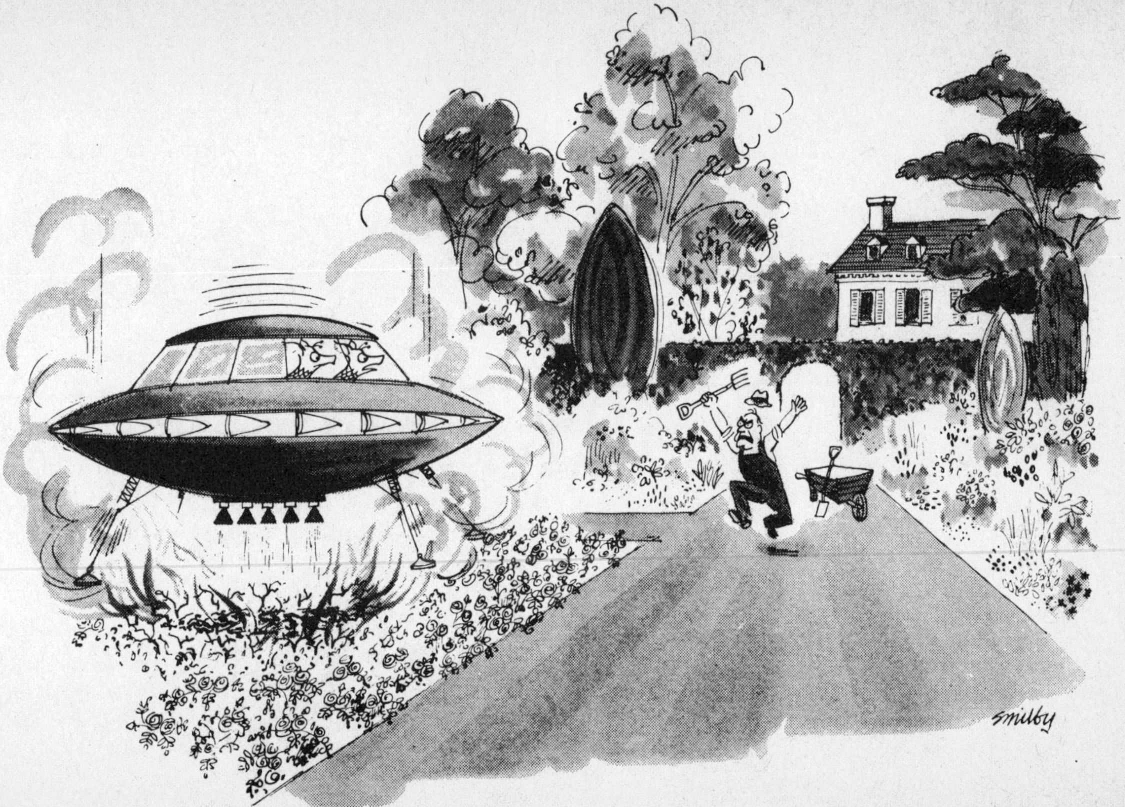

"Watch it – it looks as if they're going to be hostile."

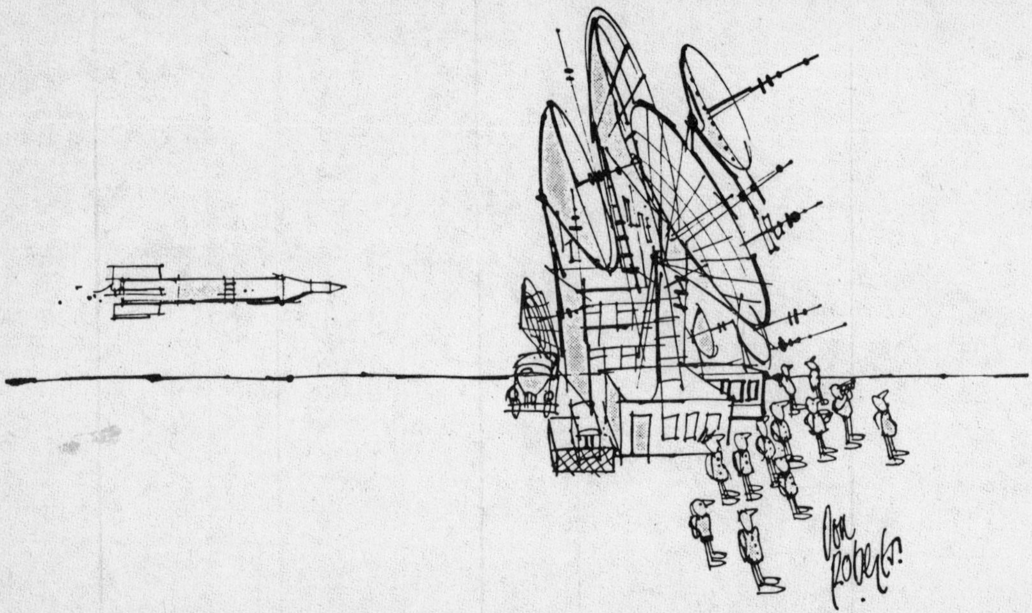

CHELM OF TRYG 2, British Space Station of the Future

by Bill Tidy

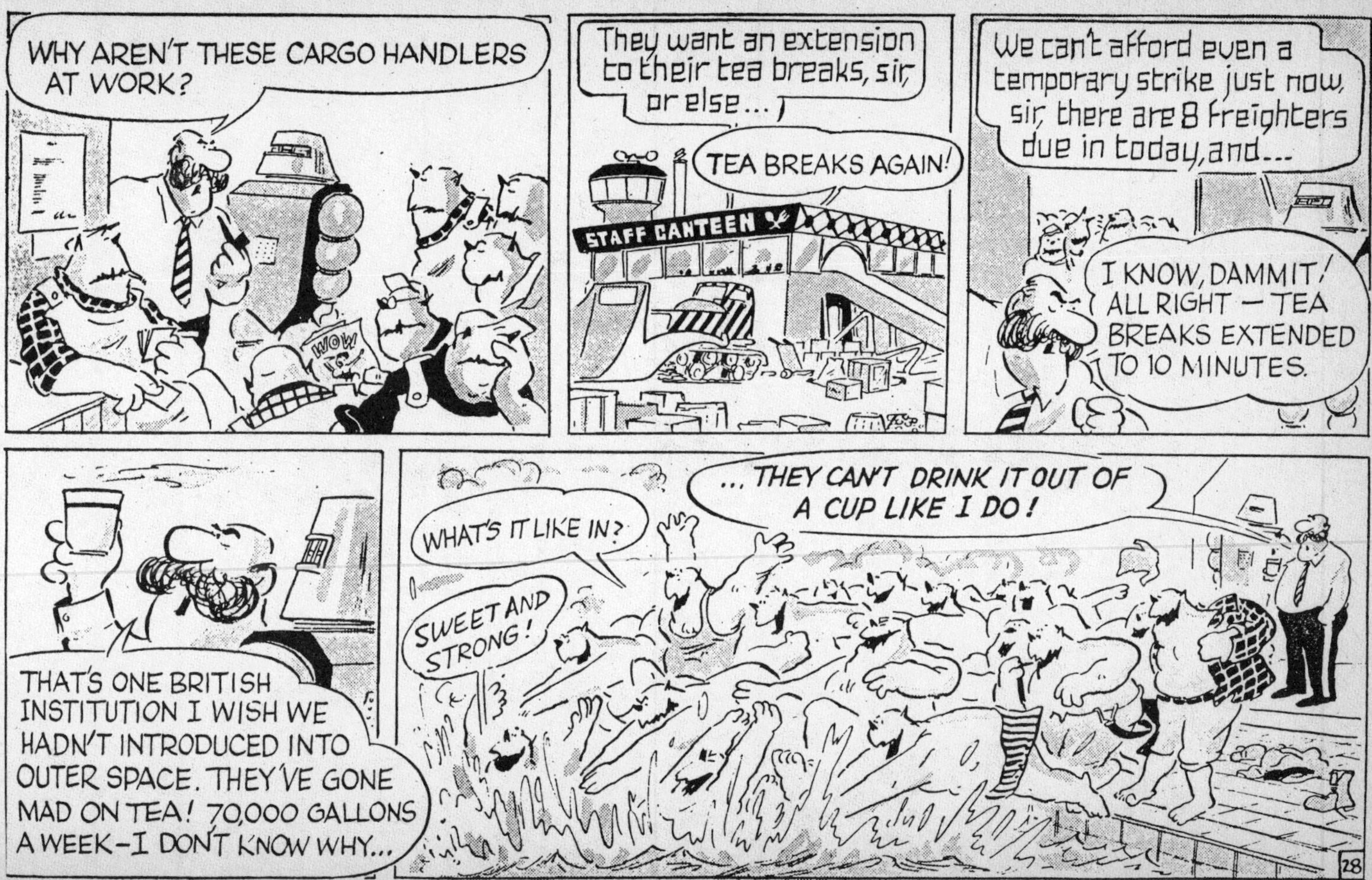

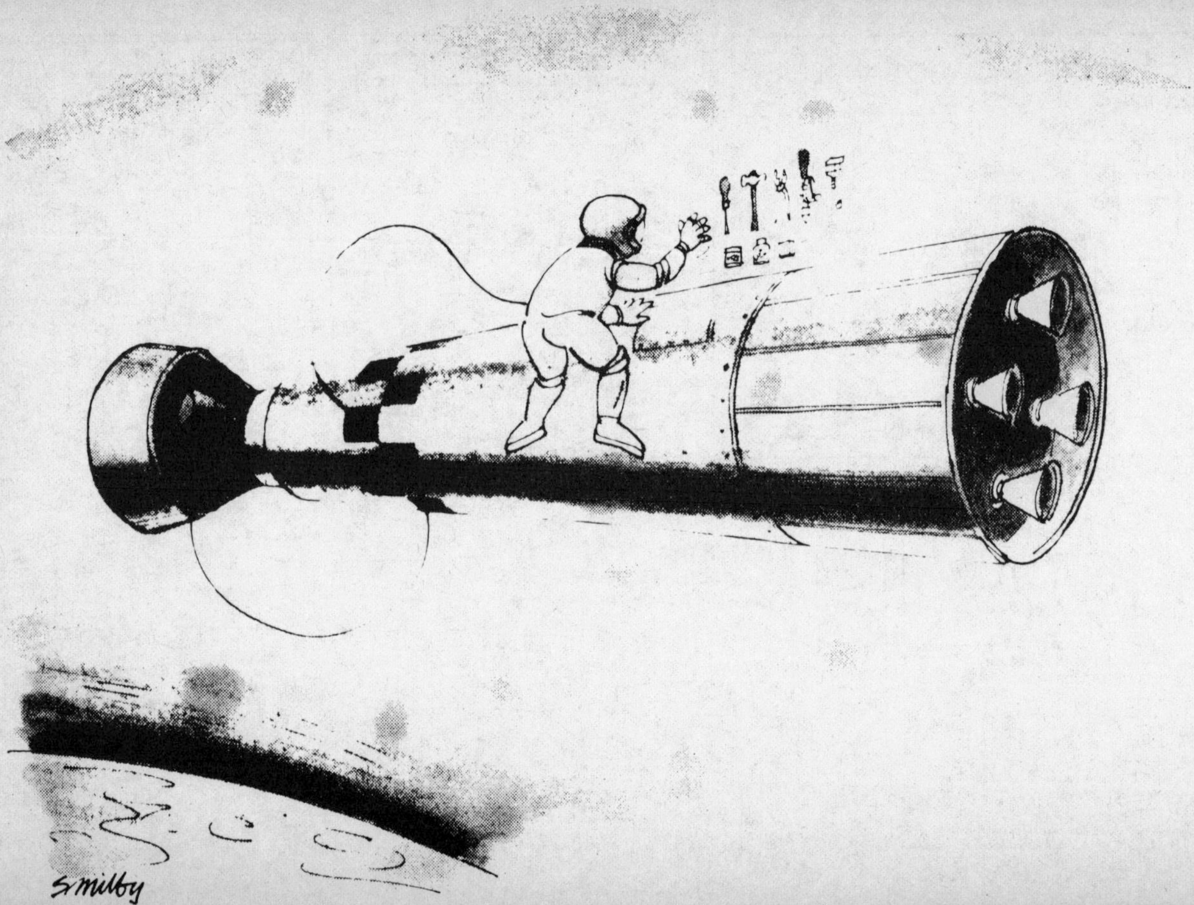
Smilby

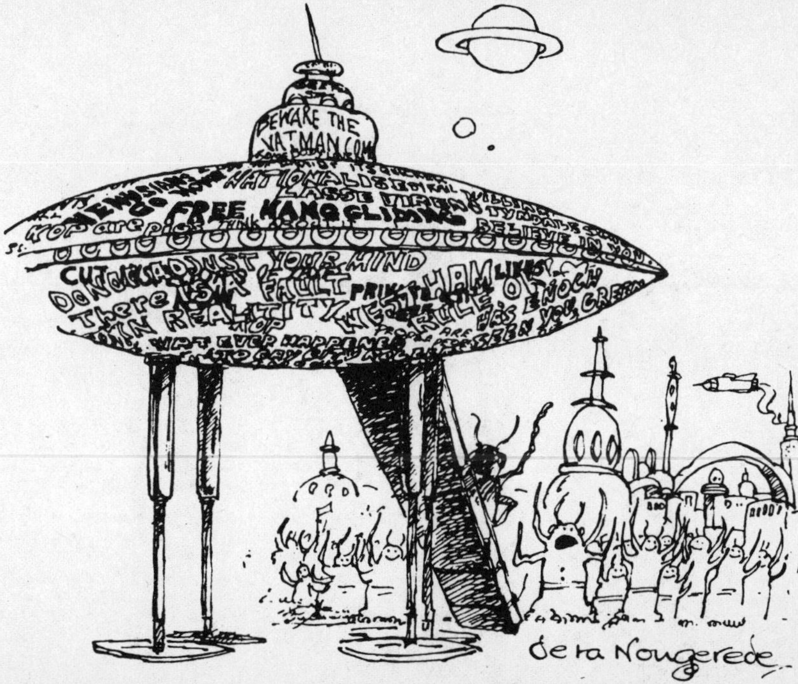

"You reached Earth, then?"

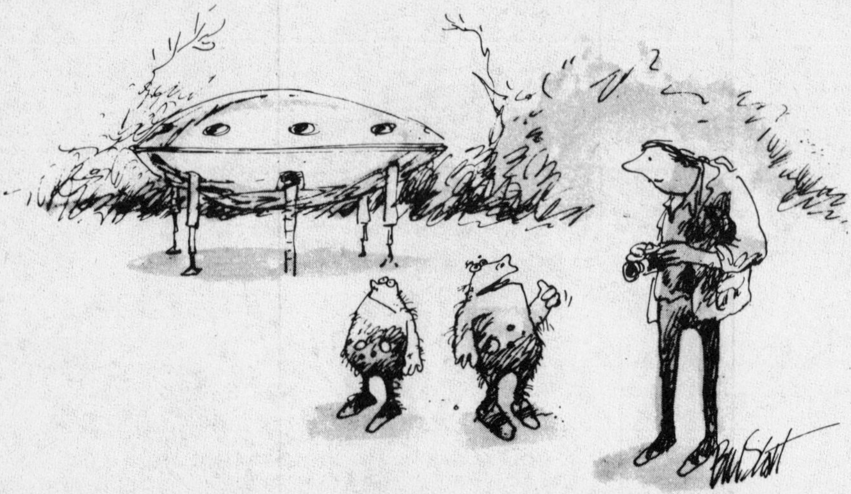

"No, no, you've got it wrong. You're much more advanced than us – in fact, the thing we came in was supposed to be a tin opener."

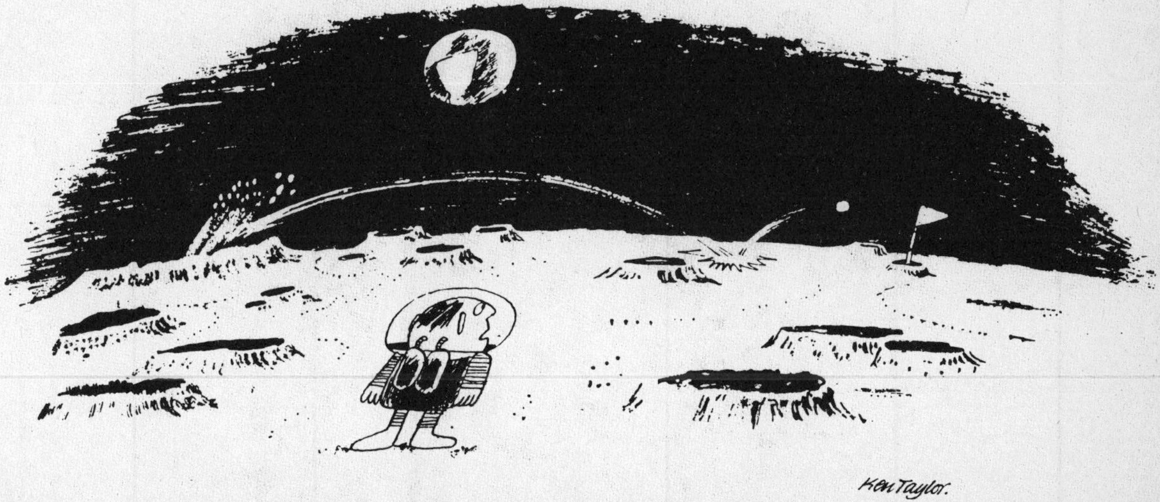
Ken Taylor.

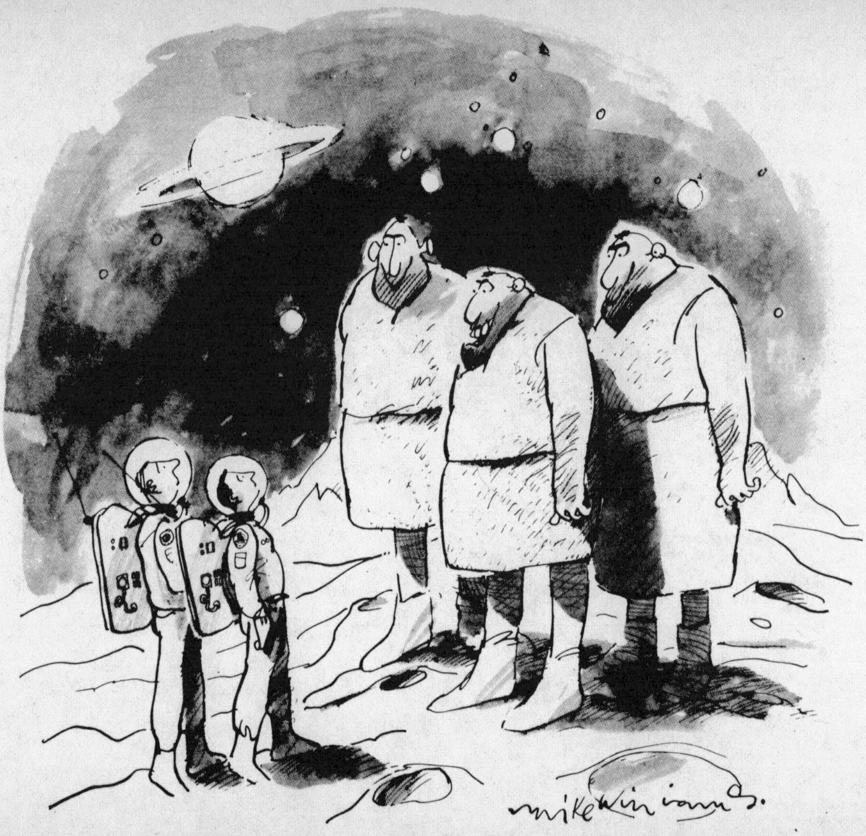

"You think we're something – you should see our menfolk!"

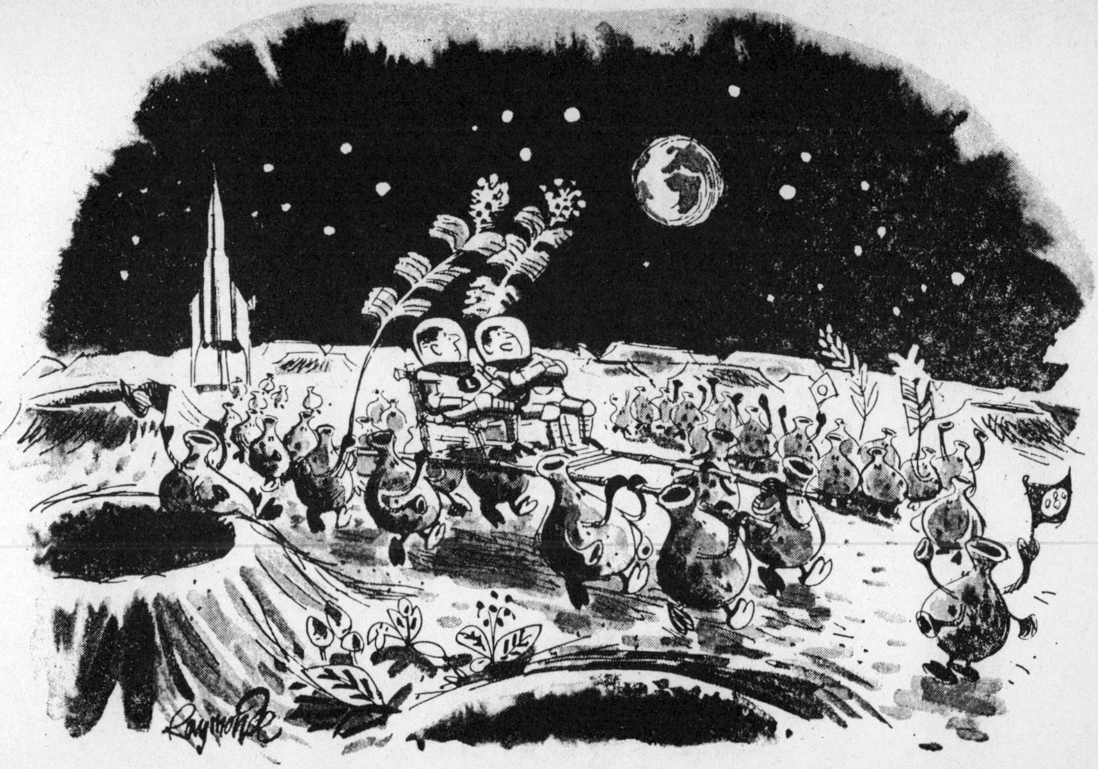

"Here we go again – conquest – subjection – insurrection – independence . . ."

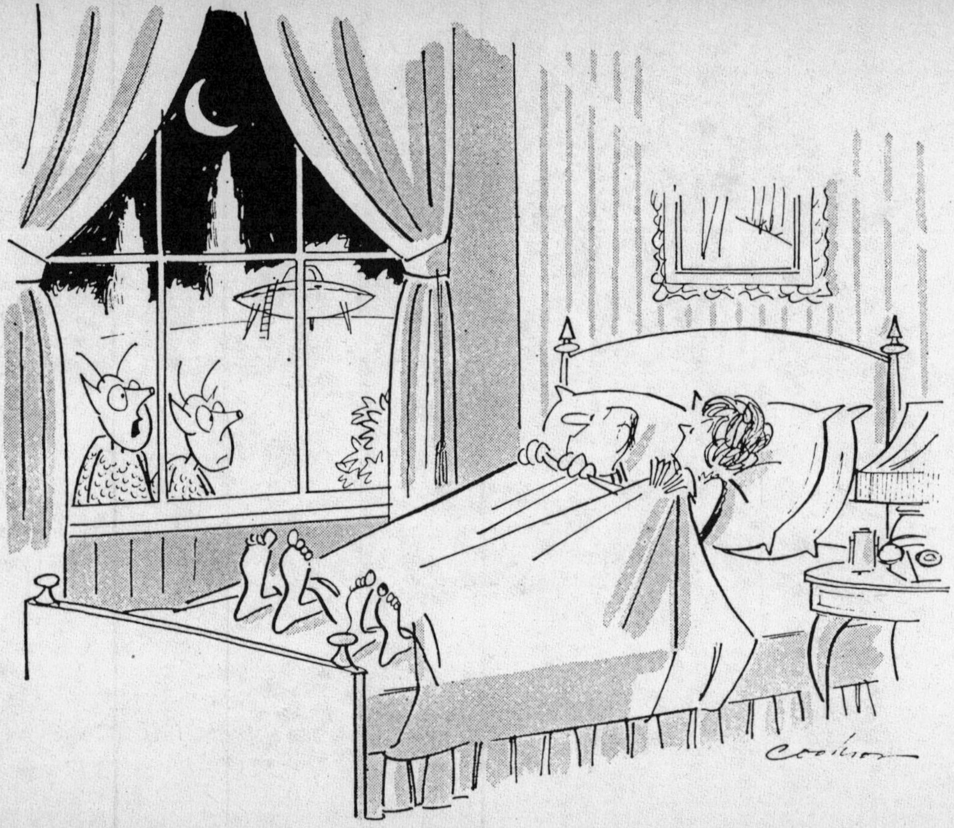

"It appears to be a two-headed quadruped."

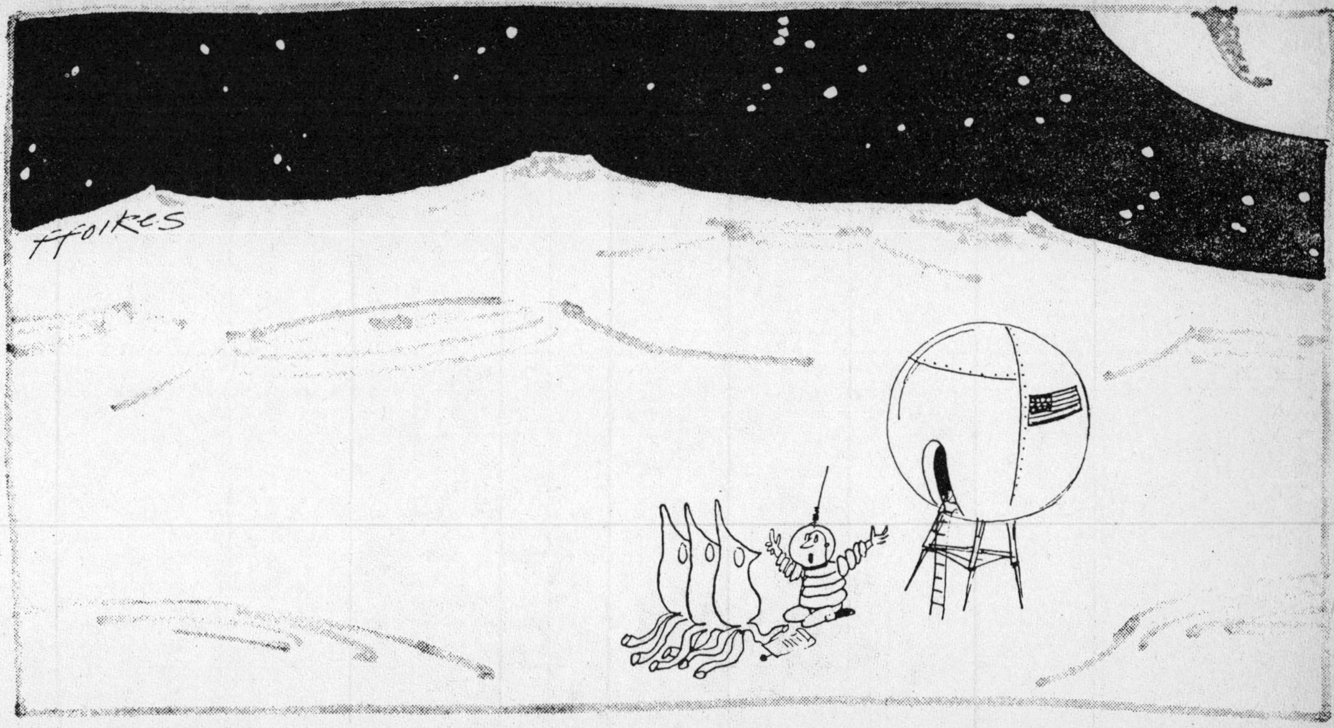

"OK, twenty-six dollars, and that's two dollars more than we paid for Manhattan."

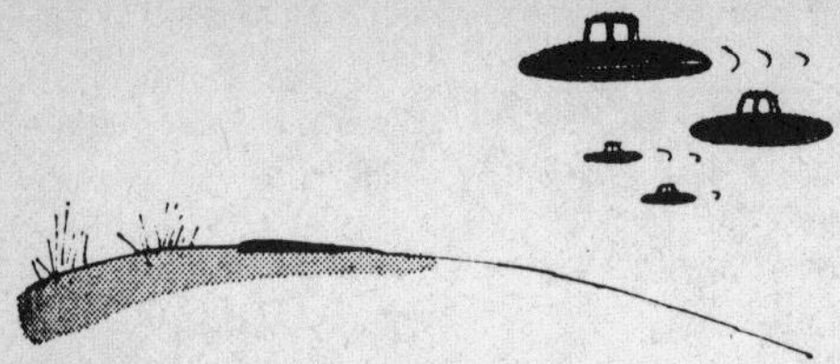

"Over there . . . desolate scrubland, an ideal spot for our first base . . .

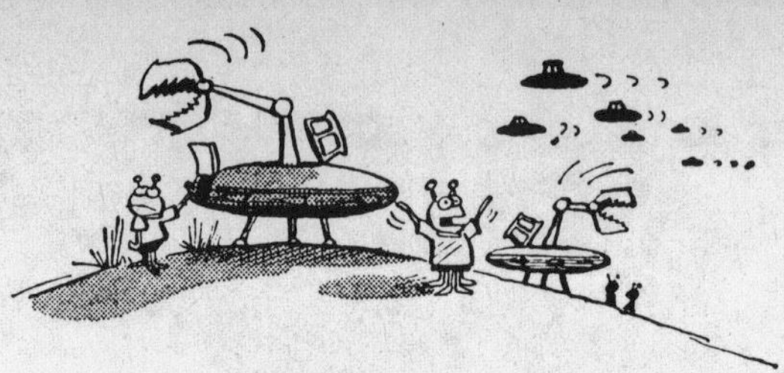

. . . I name this place 'Nubolaxy.' From here our great people will commence operations to take over the primitive earth creatures . . . start digging . . ."

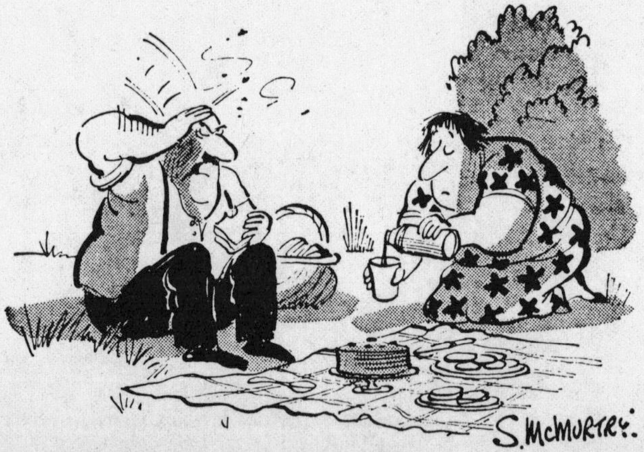

"Damned midges!"

CHELM OF TRYG 2, British Space Station of the Future

by Bill Tidy

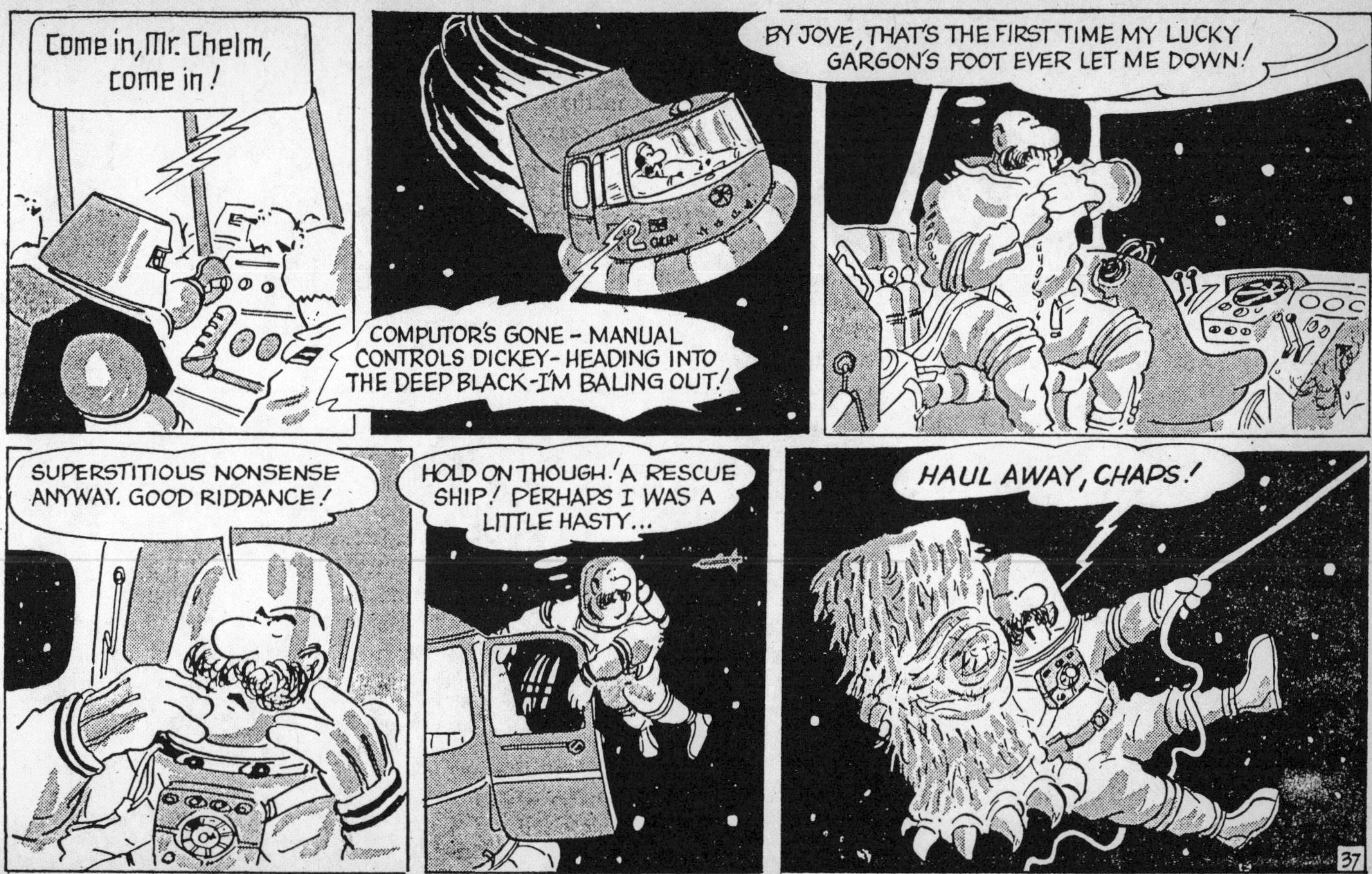

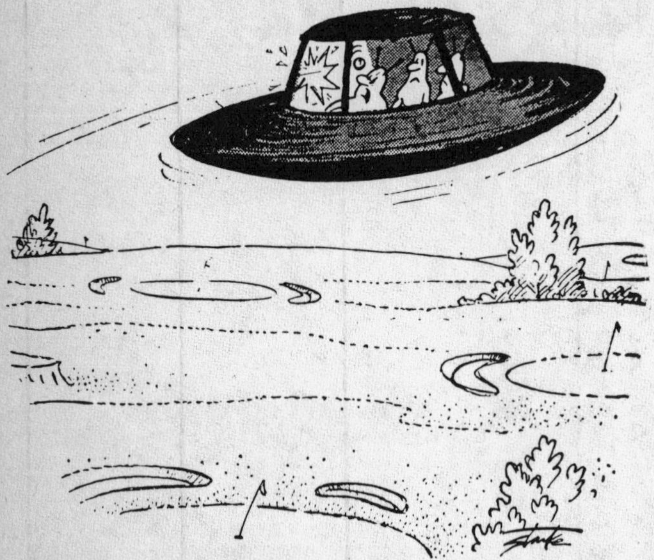

"That settles it – they're hostile!"

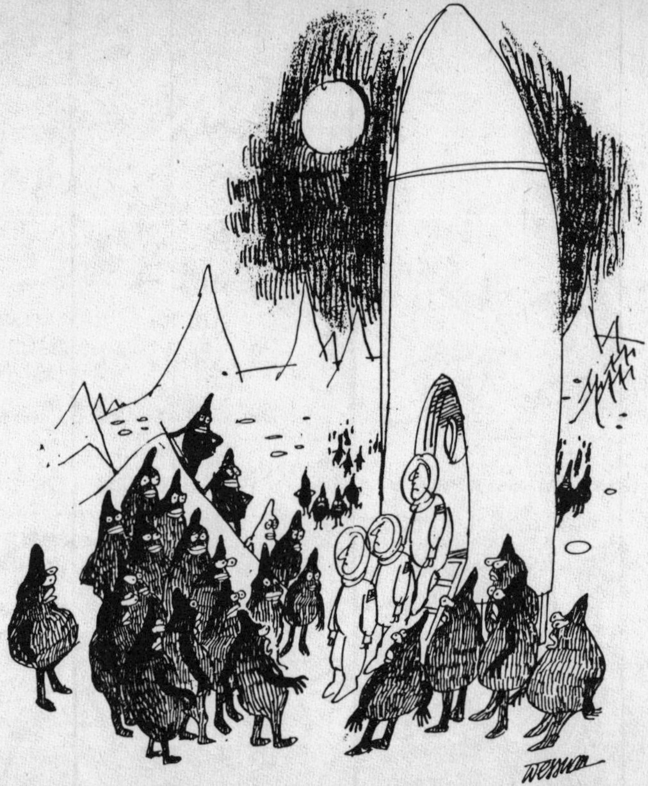

"I suppose they didn't want to risk their first-class citizens."

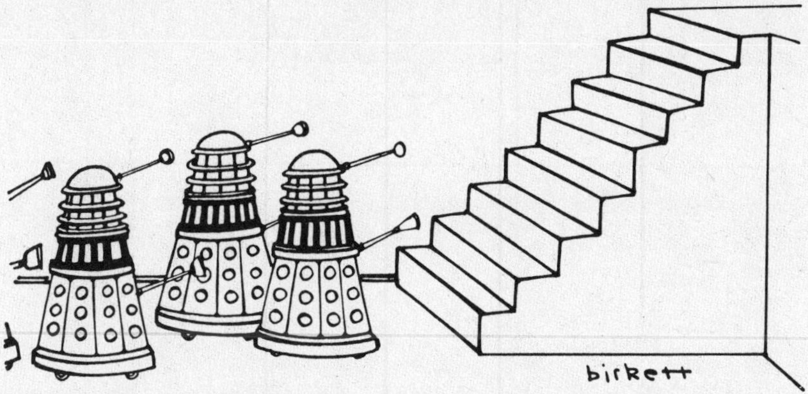

"Well, this certainly buggers our plan to conquer the Universe."

*"Third floor,
Servo motors
and liquid
fuel injection."*

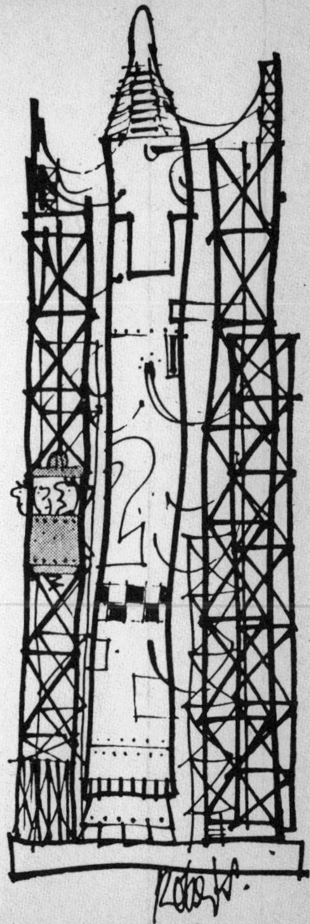

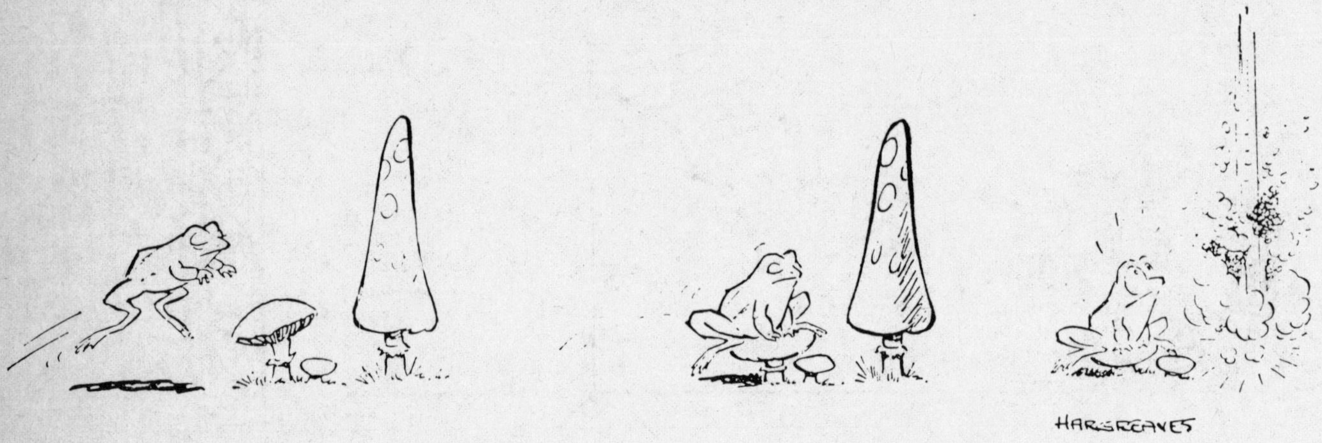
HARGREAVES

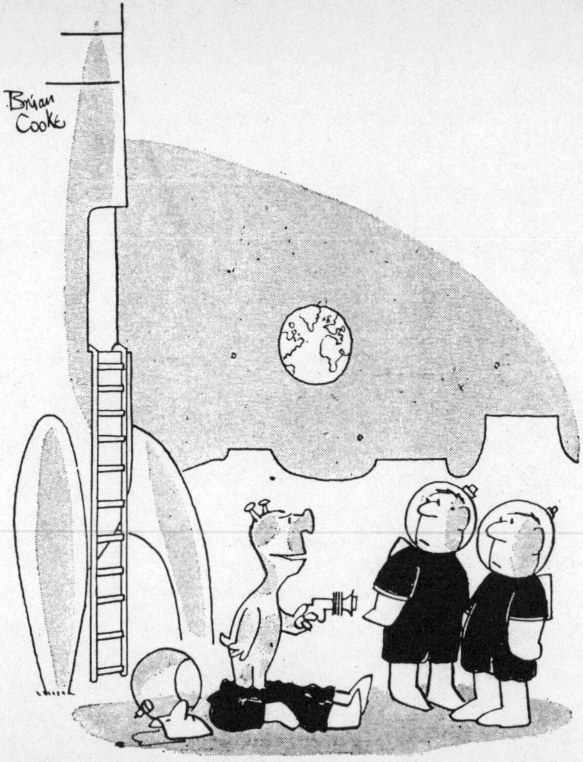

"Home at last! Okay, you guys . . . get back into the rocket!"

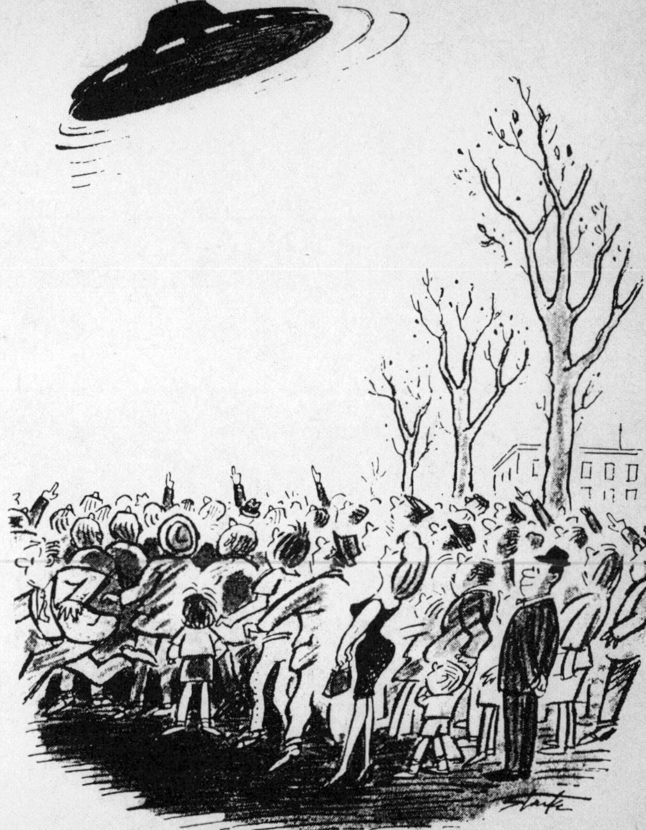

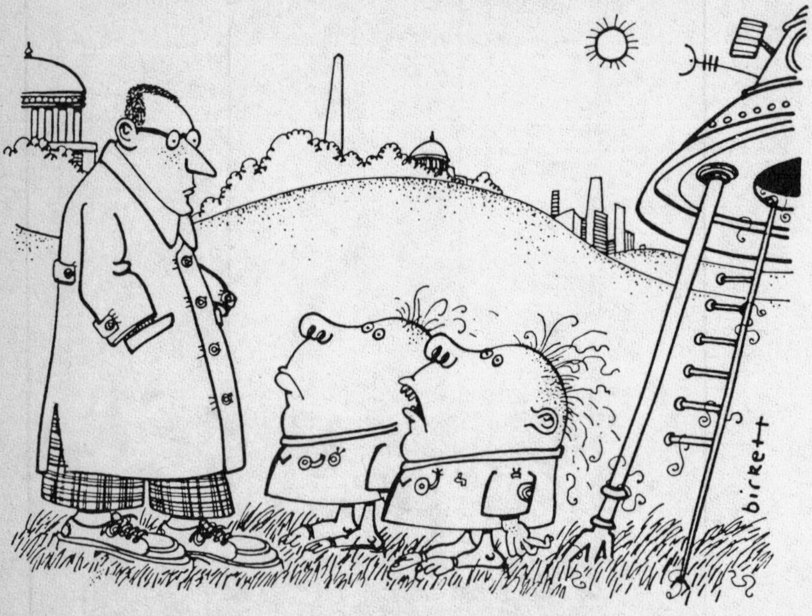

"Never mind the President – take us to his trichologist."

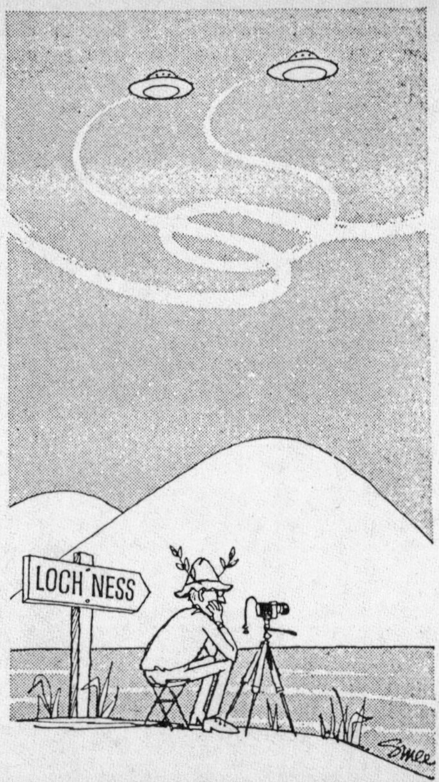

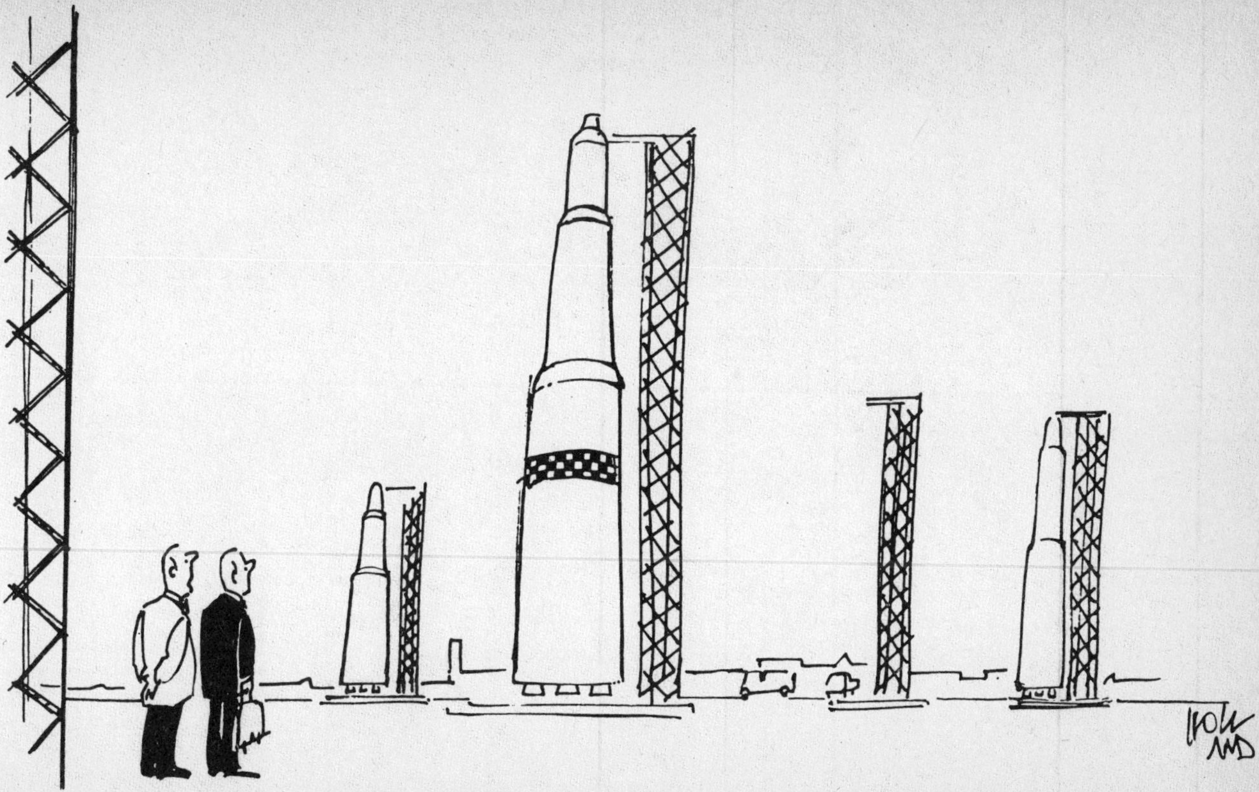

"Actually, they're spin-offs from a project to produce heat-resistant kitchenware."

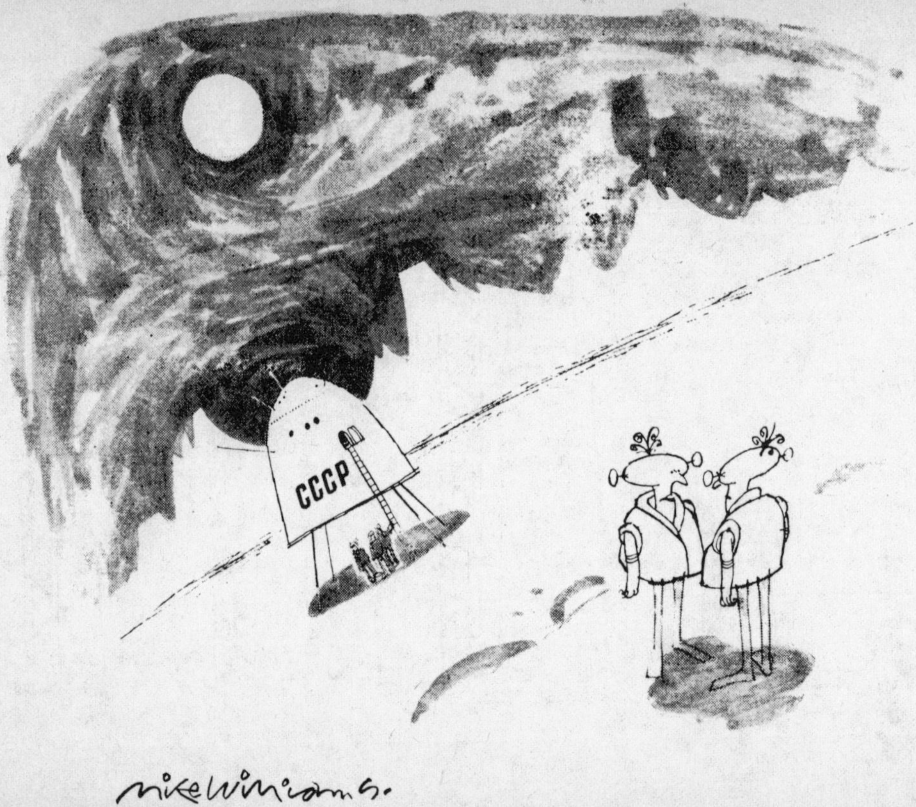

"They think they're on manoeuvres in Siberia."

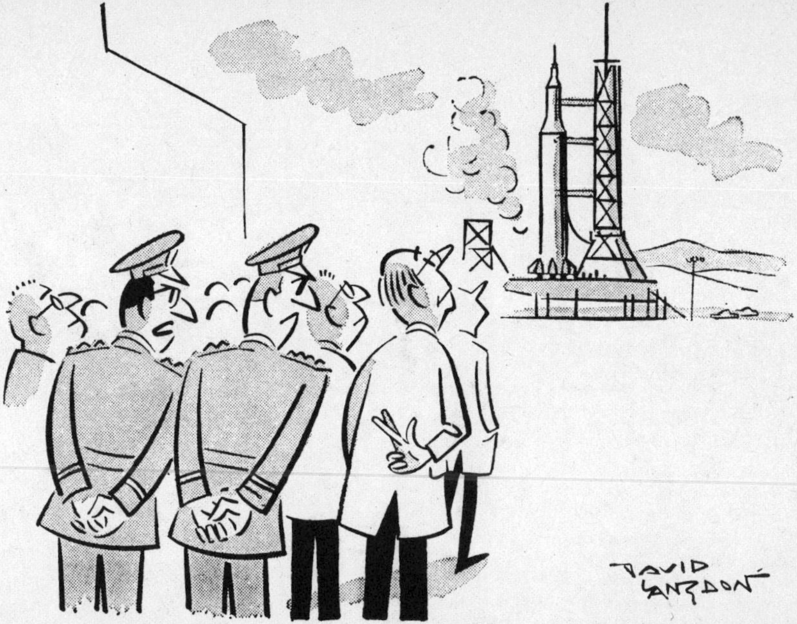

"Bit of an unscientific gesture that, after twenty-four billion dollars on research and development."

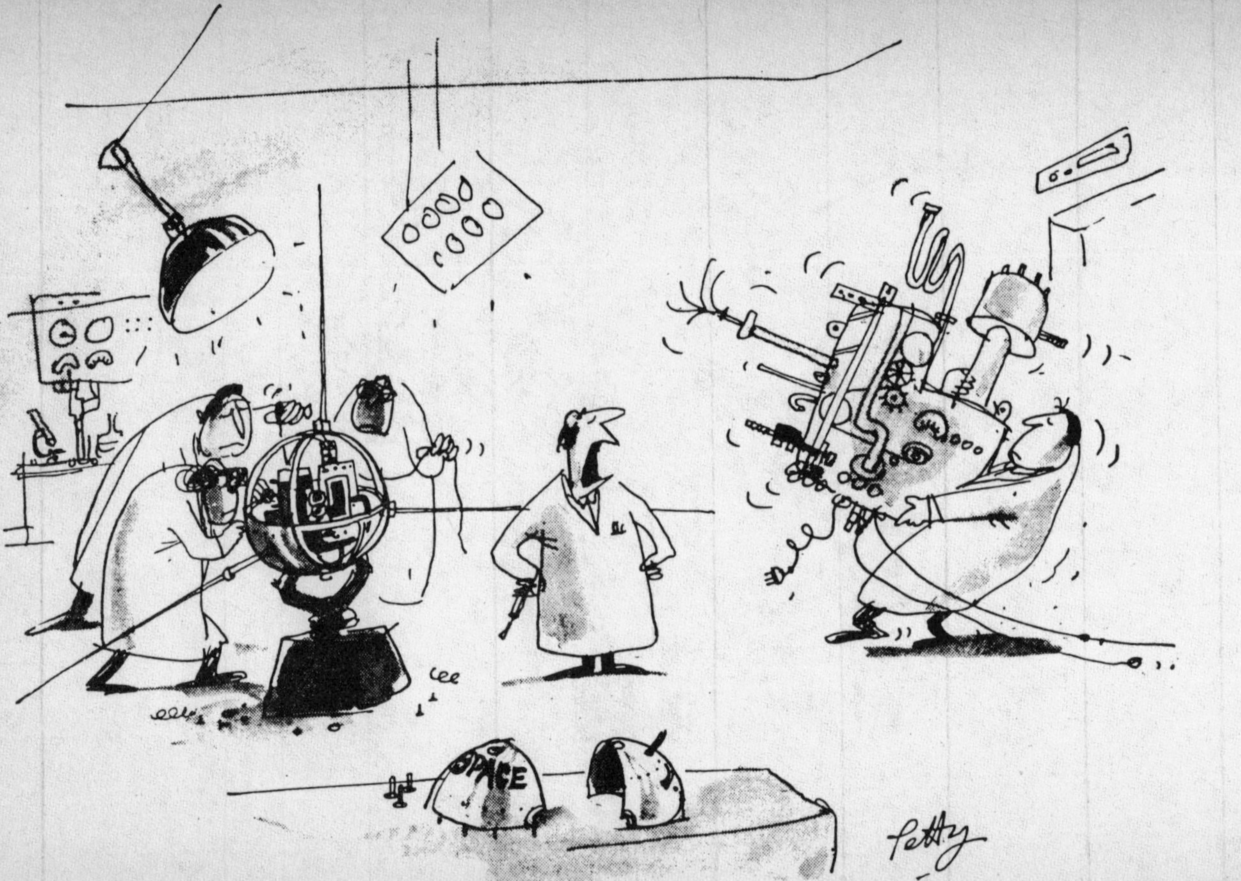

"Still too big, Perring, too big!"

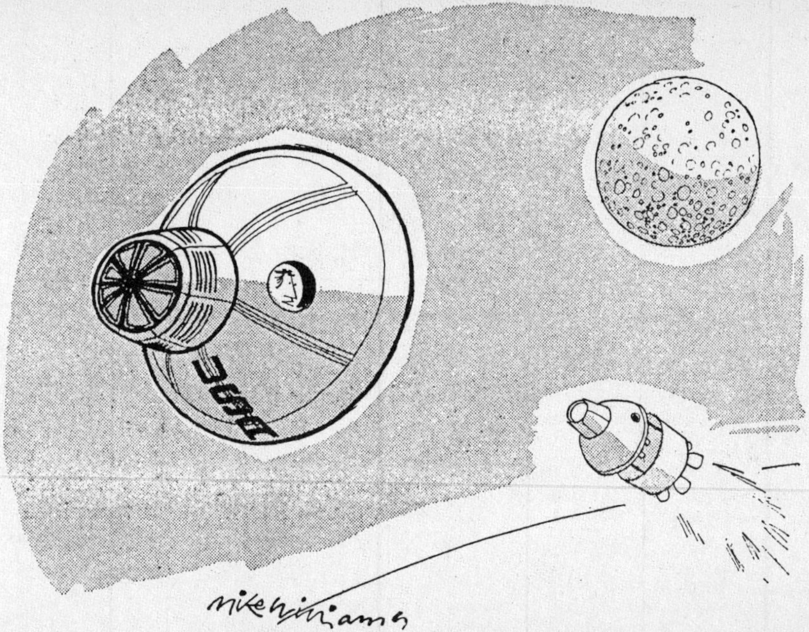

"It's either the Russians or a David Frost interview."

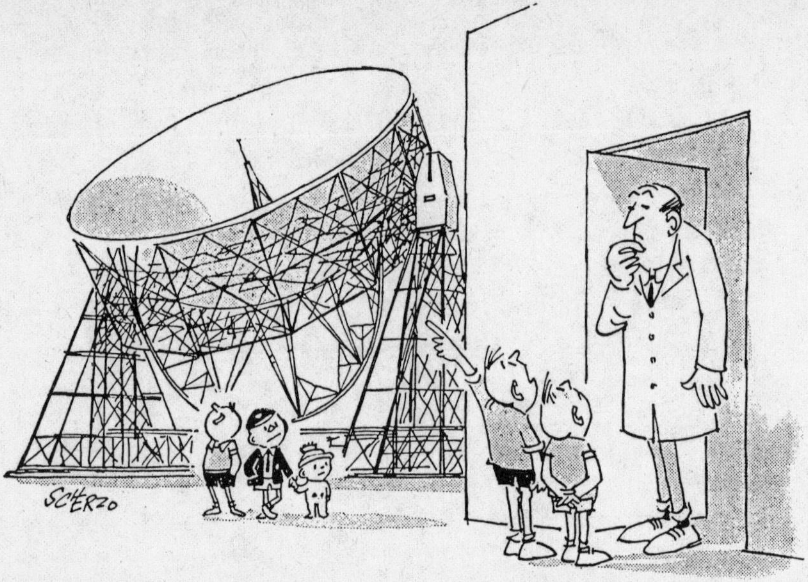

"Could we have our ball back, please?"

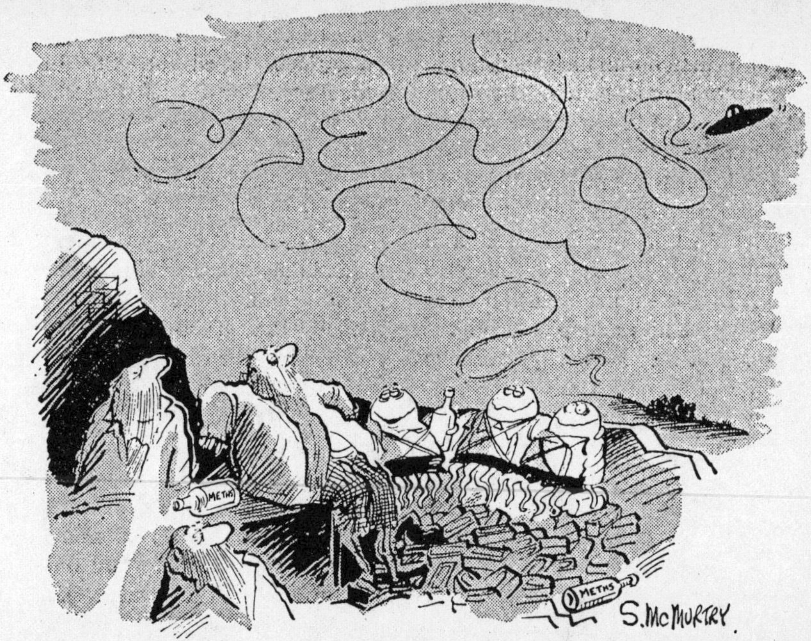

"Your King sure as hell can drive."

CHELM OF TRYG 2, British Space Station of the Future

by Bill Tidy

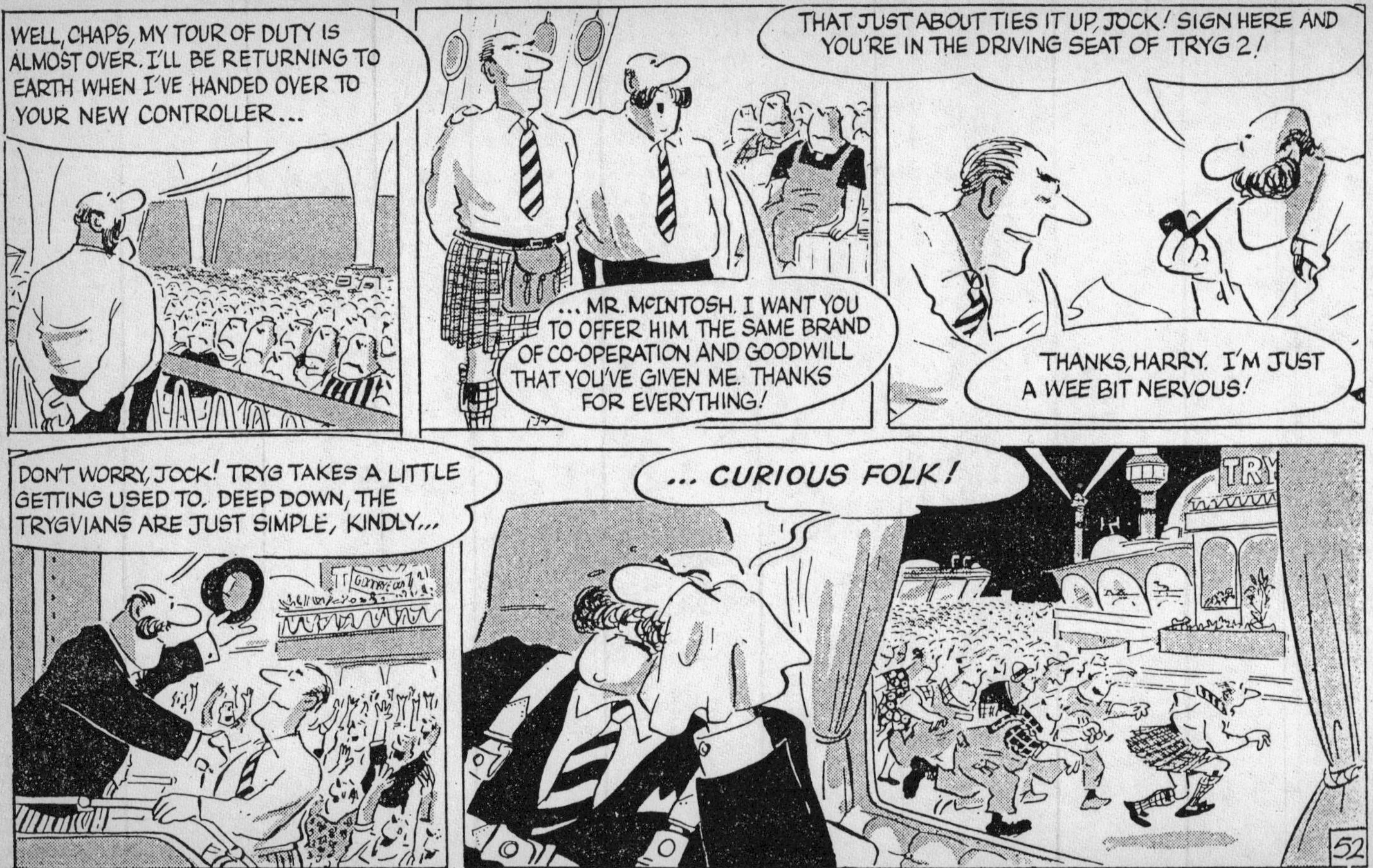

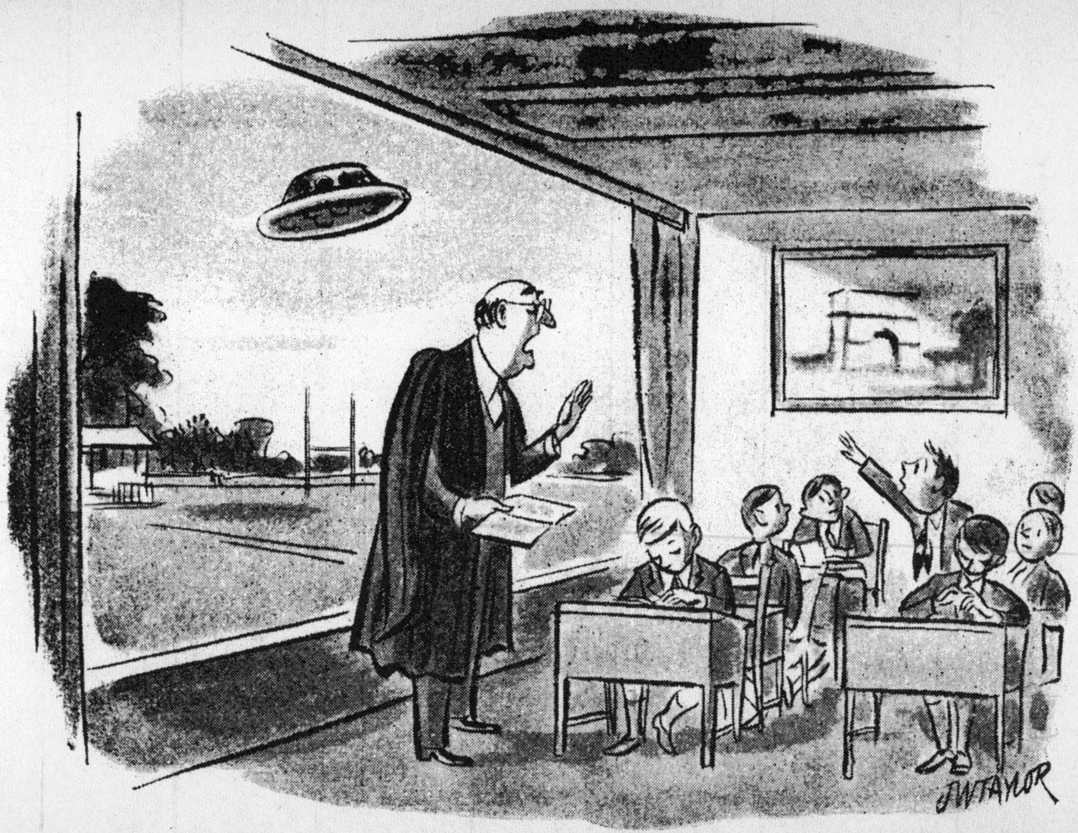

"En français, Jackson, en français."

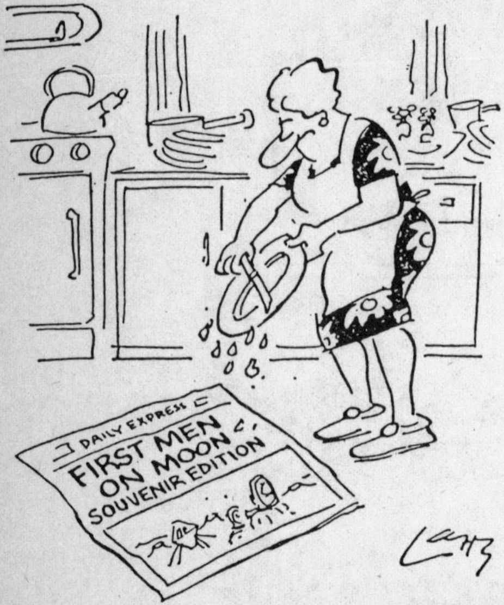

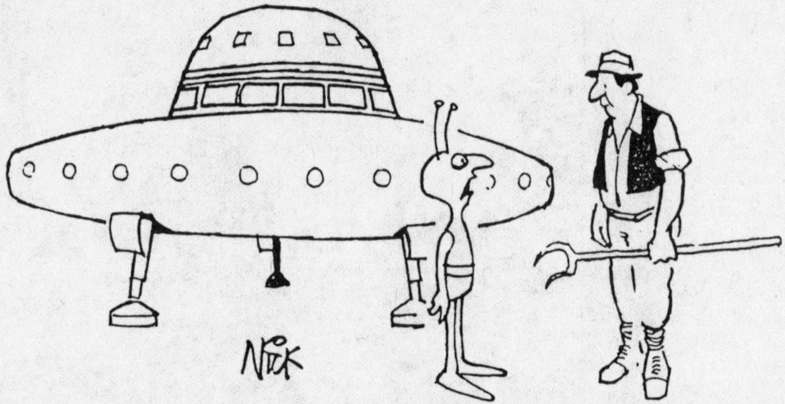

"Doesn't it make you sick? Our baggage has been sent to Jupiter."

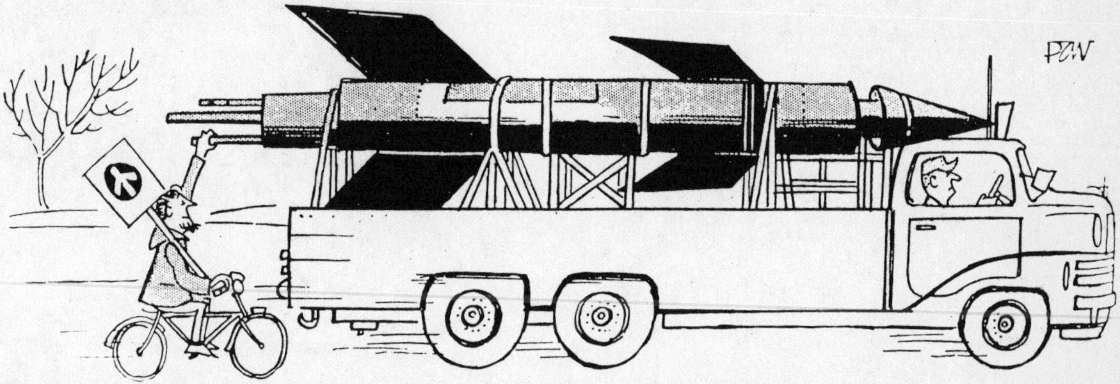

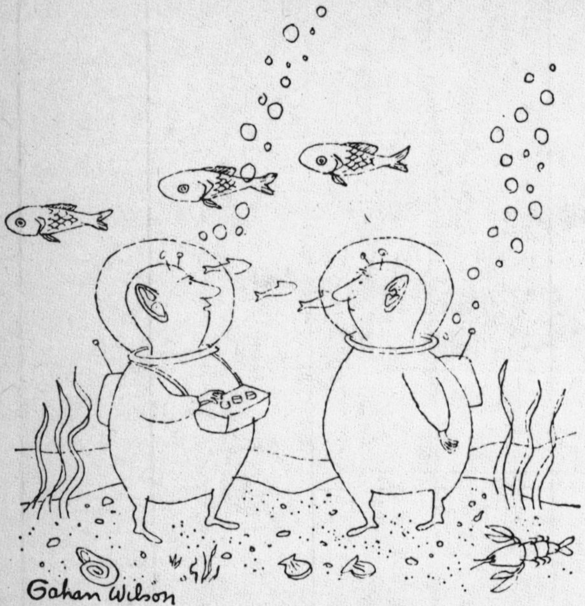

"Strange . . . Earth's atmosphere is much denser than we were told it would be."

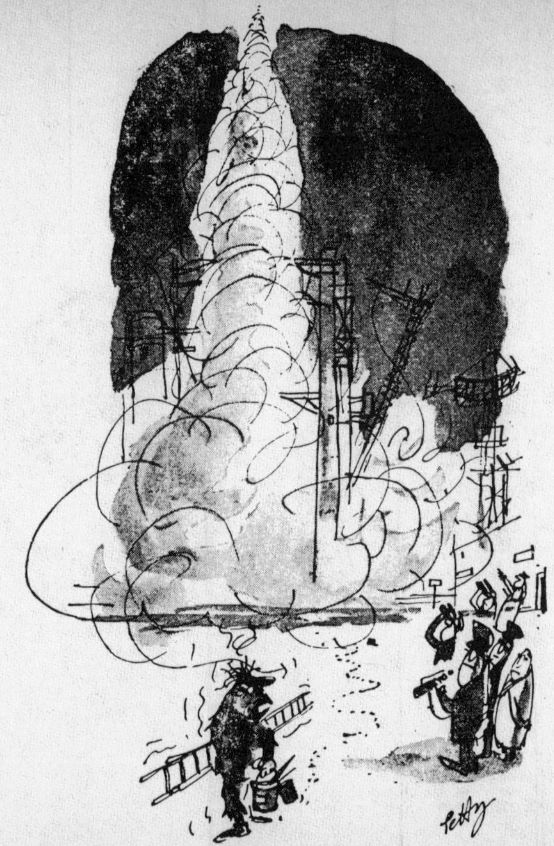

"You might like to know the number's all smudged."

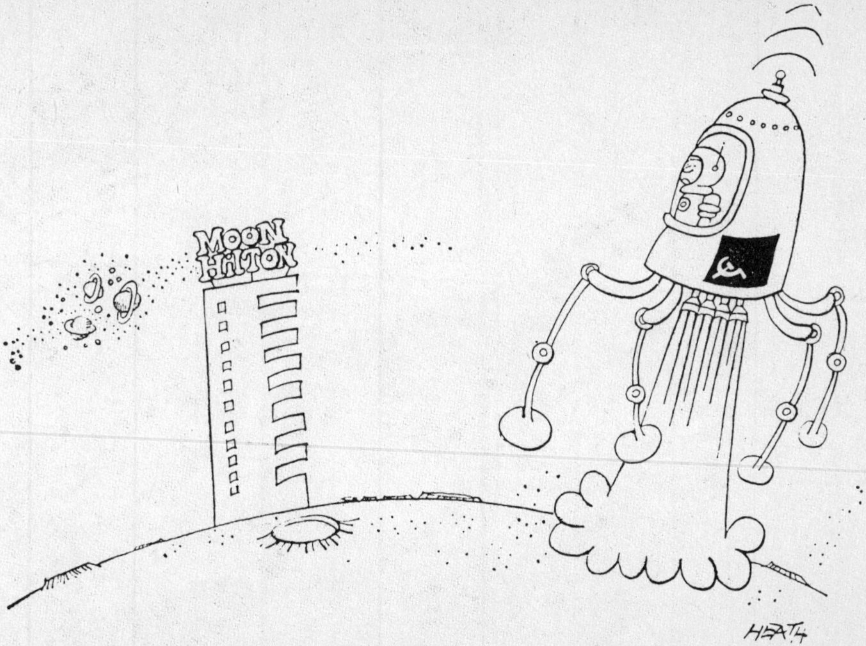
MOON HILTON
HEATH

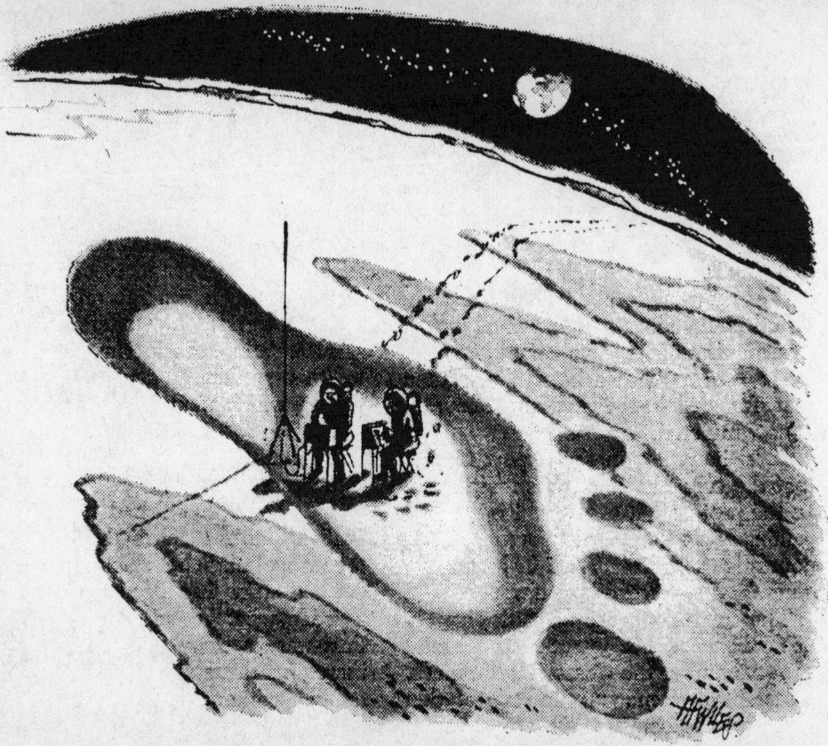

"First expedition five miles out but no sign of life yet."

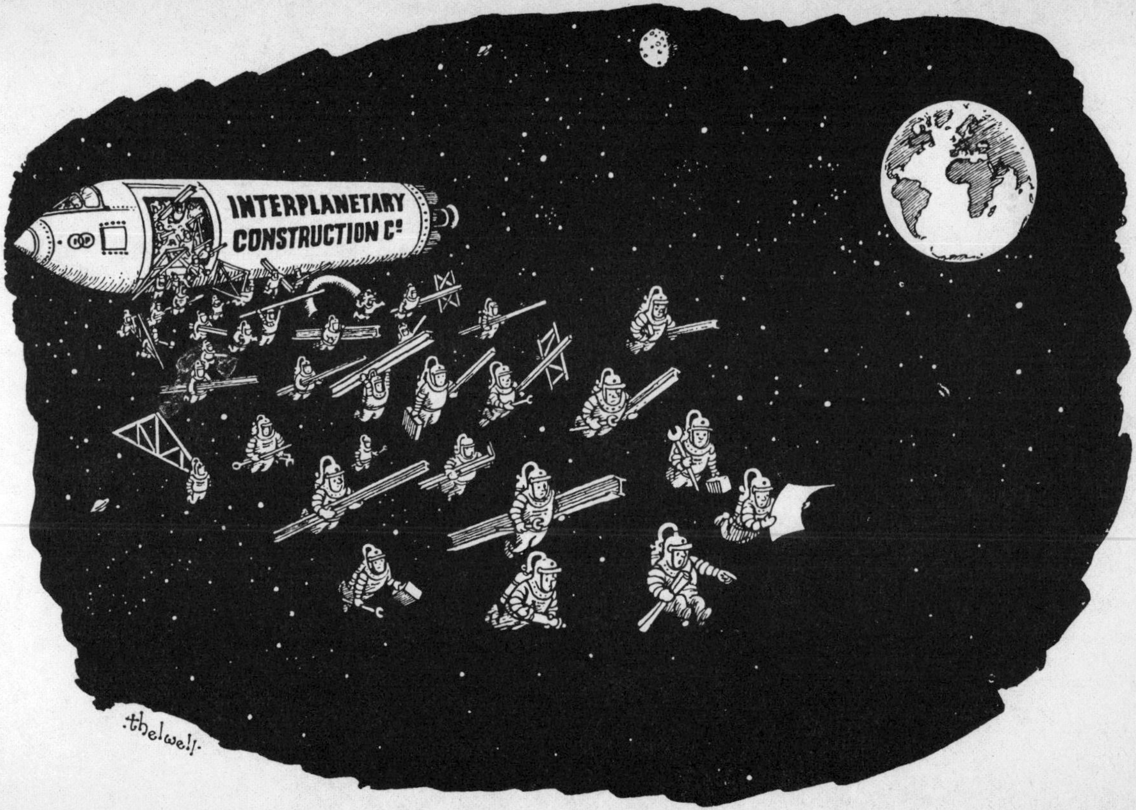

"Oh – about here, I should think."

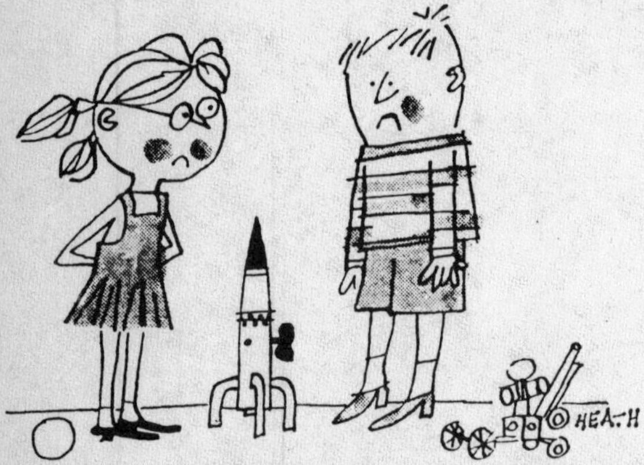

"It needs two keys to make it work, and Mum's got the other."

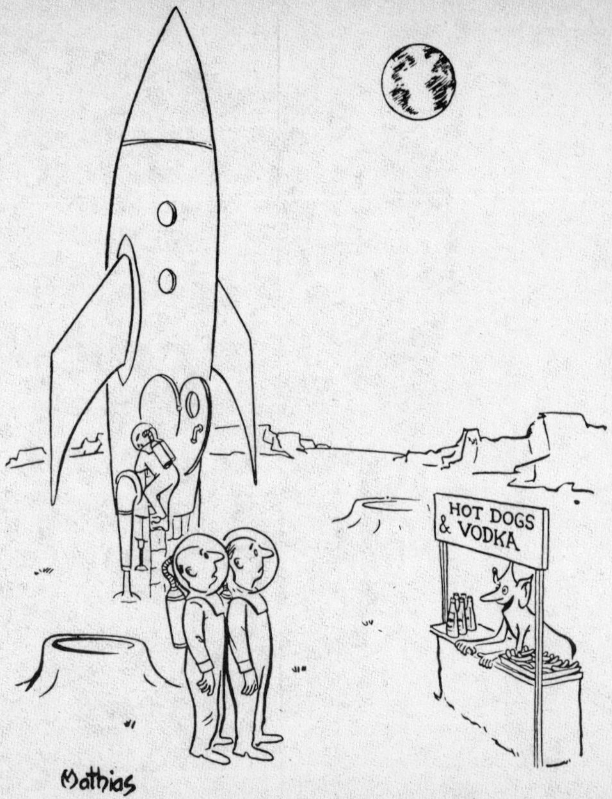

"We've been half expecting you."